From Your Friends At The MAILBO

W9-BNA-820

DECEMBER

A MONTH OF IDEAS AT YOUR FINGERTIPS!

GRADES 1–3

Jessup

WRITTEN BY

Resa Audet, Amy Barsanti, Karen Ciampa, Stacie Stone Davis, Jennifer Gibson, Nicole Iacovazzi, Carolyn Kanoy, Susie Kapaun, Pam Kucks, Jan Masengale, Sharon Murphy, Kathy Wolf

EDITED BY

Lynn Bemer Coble, Carol Rawleigh, Jennifer Rudisill, Gina Sutphin, Kathy Wolf

ILLUSTRATED BY

Jennifer Tipton Bennett, Cathy Spangler Bruce, Teresa Davidson, Clevell Harris, Susan Hodnett, Sheila Krill, Rebecca Saunders, Barry Slate, Donna K. Teal

TYPESET BY

David Jarrell, Lynette Maxwell

COVER DESIGNED BY

Jennifer Tipton Bennett

www.themailbox.com

TABLE OF CONTENTS

December Calendar

Birthday Of Bingo Month

Celebrate the birthday of bingo sometime during the month of December. Give each child a piece of construction paper on which he can draw a bingo grid. Have each child program his board to practice spelling words, math facts, or vocabulary words. After the grids have been programmed, play a few rounds of bingo. Award winning students with small stickers or pencils.

International Calendar Awareness Month

During International Calendar Awareness Month, give students practice using and reading a calendar. Provide each child with a copy of a December calendar. Have students use their calendars to answer a variety of questions such as "On what day will Christmas fall this year?" and "What is the date of the third Monday in December?"

10—Birth Date Of Melvil Dewey

Born on this date in 1851, Melvil Dewey founded the decimal library-classification system called the Dewey decimal classification. This is the most widely used method of classifying library books. Read the books *Booker's Bunch, Book 1* and *Booker's Bunch, Book 2* by Jerry J. Mallett and Marian R. Bartch (Perma-Bound Books, 1988) to help your students better understand the card catalog and the Dewey decimal system. Afterward let students use the card catalog and the Dewey decimal system to locate books of their choice.

12—Poinsettia Day

Explain that Poinsettia Day is a day set aside to enjoy poinsettias and to honor Dr. Joel Roberts Poinsett. Poinsett—an American diplomat—introduced this flower to the United States. Then show students a poinsettia that you have brought to the classroom. Show students the tiny flowers surrounded by the red, pink, yellowish, or white *bracts* (special leaves). Point out the green leaves on the poinsettia, too. Explain to students that the leaves and stem of the poinsettia can cause abdominal cramps if eaten. In addition, the plant's sap can cause skin and eye irritations. After students have had a chance to observe the poinsettia, present it as a gift to your school principal, nurse, or secretary.

14—Discovery Of The South Pole

It was on this date in 1911 that the South Pole was found by Roald Amundsen and his team. Amundsen's team consisted of four companions and 52 sled dogs. After explaining this to students, share excerpts and pictures from the book *Peary And Amundsen: Race To The Poles* by Antony Mason (Raintree Steck-Vaughn Publishers, 1995). Then survey students to determine how many of them think they might like to visit the South Pole.

17—Wright Brothers Day

Explain that on this date in 1903, brothers Wilbur and Orville Wright flew the first powered airplane. Their flights heralded a new age of transportation. Read the book *Wilbur And Orville And The Flying Machine* by Max Marquardt (Raintree Publishers, 1989). Then have each student pretend to be a news reporter covering the events at Kitty Hawk, North Carolina. After students have written news reports describing the first flight, allow volunteers to read their stories; then bind the stories into a classroom collection titled "First Flight By The Wrights."

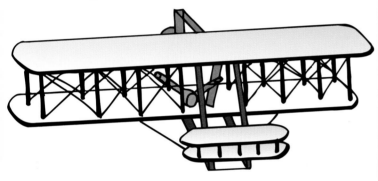

California Kiwifruit Day
(Annually, The First Day Of Winter)

This day is set aside to educate Americans about the nutritional benefits of kiwifruit, ways to enjoy kiwifruit, and the history of kiwifruit. Get your students interested in this tasty fruit by allowing them to sample a piece. Cut each of several kiwifruits into slices and give each child a slice. After each child has had a taste, survey students to find out how many of them liked the kiwifruit. Then compare the taste of the kiwifruit to other fruits such as strawberries.

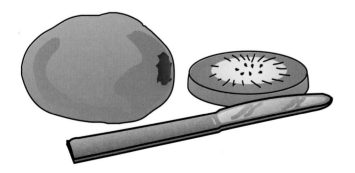

19—Birth Date Of Eve Bunting

Celebrate this author's birthday by sharing *The Wednesday Surprise* (Clarion Books, 1989). In this story, much to her family's surprise, a young girl teaches her grandmother to read. After reading ask students to name other things that children can teach older persons, such as computer skills or how to play a video game.

31—Make Up Your Mind Day

This day is set aside for all people who have a difficult time making up their minds. Introduce this topic by talking about times when you've had a difficult time making up your mind and playact one of these situations, if desired. Then let students practice their decision-making skills with this activity. On each of several index cards, print situations for which a decision is needed. Then, one at a time, read aloud a situation. Ask students to think about what decision they would make and why. Allow volunteers to share their decisions. Discuss with students the consequences associated with each decision made.

CLASSROOM TIMES

Teacher:_____ Date: _____

DECEMBER

Events

Reminders

Superstars

Special Thanks

Help Wanted

Goodness, Gracious! It's Gingerbread!

The scrumptious smell of spicy gingerbread is sure to get your students' attention. Try these tempting treats and ideas to reinforce skills across the curriculum.

ideas by Nicole Iacovazzi

Gingerbread Graphing

Read aloud *The Gingerbread Boy* by Paul Galdone (Clarion Books, 1979). Discuss how the old woman made the gingerbread boy with flour, water, and spices. On the board, help children list some of the ingredients used in gingerbread. Pass around spice containers of ground ginger, allspice, cinnamon, and cloves for students to sniff. Ask children if they have smelled warm gingerbread right out of the oven. Have them name some mouthwatering adjectives to describe gingerbread.

Then tempt students' taste buds with this graphing idea. As a class, make gingerbread men together using the recipe below. Or bake them ahead of time and provide one gingerbread man for each child.

For graphing practice, provide each child with a copy of the reproducible record sheet on page 12. Next give each child a gingerbread cookie and tell him to take only ONE BITE out of it. Together record the results of the gingerbread tasting. Graph which part of the gingerbread cookie was eaten first—head, arm, foot, or body. Determine which part was the most commonly eaten and the least commonly eaten. Finally allow children to enjoy the rest of their gingerbread cookies!

Gingerbread Cookies

1 1/2 c. molasses	1 tsp. cinnamon
1 c. packed brown sugar	2/3 c. cold water
1 tsp. allspice	1/3 c. shortening
6 1/2 c. flour	1 tsp. cloves
2 tsp. ginger	

Mix together molasses, brown sugar, water, and shortening. Add all other ingredients and cover for 2 hours. Heat oven to 350°F. On a floured surface, roll out dough until it is 1/4" thick. Cut out gingerbread men with cookie cutters and place them on a greased cookie sheet. Bake 10 minutes and cool. Decorate with frosting, raisins for eyes, and red cinnamon candies for buttons if desired.

Save The Gingerbread Boy!

In *The Gingerbread Boy* by Paul Galdone, the quick but arrogant cookie-boy is eaten when he is outsmarted by a fox. Of course gingerbread boys are made to be eaten, but what if this one got away? After reading the book, have your students name ways to rescue the Gingerbread Boy from the fox. Then engage students in this follow-up activity that results in a clever bulletin-board display.

To prepare for the activity, write the letter on chart paper. Fold the letter and place it in a large envelope addressed to your class. Open the envelope in front of the students and read the letter together. Ask students to think of new endings for the story in which the Gingerbread Boy survives. Then, in reply to the letter, have students write their own stories in which the Gingerbread Boy is saved from the fox.

To create a bulletin board, enlarge, color, and cut out the pattern on page 11 to make a large Gingerbread Boy. Mount it in the center of a bulletin board along with the letter. Add student stories and the title "Save The Gingerbread Boy!" Your students and guests will enjoy reading these happy endings!

Dear Friend,
I hear that you've read my story! I just wanted to tell you that the ending is all wrong. I was never meant to be eaten by that tricky fox! Please help me!
Can you please write my story a new way so that I DON'T get eaten in the end? I want to be able to play with all my gingerbread friends! I hope you can save me! Thanks!

Your pal,
The Gingerbread Boy

Run, Run, As Fast As You Can!

In the story of *The Gingerbread Boy*, there is a continuing pattern of the Gingerbread Boy being chased by different characters who claim they can catch him. After reading the story, discuss the recurring words and phrases. Ask students to name the characters and list them as they appear in the story from start to finish. Then have the class summarize each event with a brief sentence (for example: The gingerbread boy was chased by a cow.). Write the sentences in order on the board.

Next divide the class into pairs. Assign each pair a sentence to write on a sheet of drawing paper and then illustrate. When the illustrations have been completed, have partners hang their pages in order on a clothesline across the room. Have students use the sequence of events to help them retell the story.

Down The Gingerbread Path

This activity reinforces mapping skills and encourages recall of *The Gingerbread Boy*. To prepare students for mapping the adventures of the Gingerbread Boy, provide the reproducible on page 14 for each student to complete.

To stimulate creative thinking, ask each student to think of a new adventure for the Gingerbread Boy. Ask students, "Who or what might our nimble cookie-hero meet at the zoo, at the circus, on a camping trip, or at an amusement park?"

Provide drawing paper for each student to create his own adventure map. Have each student draw the places to which his Gingerbread Boy traveled. Tell each student to draw arrows to show the sequence in which the Gingerbread Boy visited these places. Then have students trade maps. As the storyteller describes his "Adventures Of Gingerbread Boy," the listener follows the arrows. Now that's a path to success!

The Gingerbread Boy Search

Who can catch the Gingerbread Boy? Maybe your students can! Help your class learn to write details and follow directions with this cooperative lesson. Use the pattern on page 11 to make several gingerbread-boy cutouts. Divide the students into groups and give each group a gingerbread-boy cutout. Ask each group to hide its gingerbread boy in your classroom, then write directions explaining how the gingerbread boy can be found. Collect the directions from all groups.

A search for the Gingerbread Boy can now begin! Redistribute the directions. In turn, have each group read the directions aloud and locate the hidden cutout. After all groups find the Gingerbread Boy's hiding places, discuss what makes a good set of directions.

Conversations With A Cookie

For some critical-thinking and creative-writing practice, have each student interview the Gingerbread Boy or another character from the story. Ask students, "If you were a news reporter interviewing the Gingerbread Boy today, what question would you ask? What would you ask the horse, the fox, or another character in the story?" Have each student think of one question for a character and write it on an index card. Collect the cards and redistribute them to other students in the class.

Provide a piece of drawing paper for each student to illustrate the character and write the answer to the question in a speech bubble. Finally, share the questions and responses. Your students will be anxious to hear from each character and discover the real scoop from these eye witnesses. Was anyone surprised when this clever cookie stepped gingerly onto the fox's back?

Units Of Gingerbread Measurement

Students are sure to love this sweet, hands-on approach to determining area and perimeter! Give each student a copy of the reproducible on page 13 and one cup of each of the following in individual zippered plastic bags: mini marshmallows, cinnamon hearts, jelly beans, and raisins. The student finds the area and perimeter of the gingerbread boy using each of the items. Each child records his answers on the grid. This activity helps students learn that it takes fewer large units than small units to cover an area or outline a shape (perimeter). Students can measure the sweetness of this activity when they complete the center and munch on their candies.

A Gem Of A Gingerbread Man

Give your students practice with learning the soft sound of *g*, as in *gingerbread*. Lead your students in a discussion of the two sounds that *g* can make: *g* as in *gas* and *g* as in *gingerbread*. Brainstorm a list of words that contain the soft sound of *g*, such as *gem, gel, gerbil, general, George, gym,* and *gentle* and write them on the board. Then give each student a brown, construction-paper copy of the pattern on page 11. Ask each child to cut out the gingerbread man and write soft *g* words on it. Allow students to work in small groups or with a buddy to find more words with the soft *g* sound.

idea contributed by Alma Hoffman

Ginger People

For a lesson in cooperation, divide students into pairs to make life-sized gingerbread people! Provide each student with a sheet of butcher paper large enough for him to lie on with arms and legs extended as his partner draws an outline of his body. Each student cuts out his shape and decorates it to make a ginger person. Provide marshmallows, licorice, raisins, and buttons. Have each child name his or her person and write the name on a nametag. Display all of the ginger people outside your door to greet visitors!

Gingerbread Production Company

To culminate your unit, invite parents or another class to a performance of *The Gingerbread Boy*. Choose one or more students for the role of narrator and assign the parts of the old man, the old woman, the cow, the horse, the threshers, the mowers, and the fox. Provide props for the characters such as an apron for the old woman, a cap for the old man, straw hats and kerchiefs for the mowers and threshers, rakes for the threshers, a cowbell for the cow, a yarn mane for the horse, and a marabou tail for the fox. The gingerbread boy may be dressed in brown pants and shirt. Staple white-paper cuffs around his wrists and ankles. After repeated practice, students will be ready to put on a production of the story. Invite parents or another class to a performance of *The Gingerbread Boy*. For a tasty finale, serve gingerbread cookies to all! (See the recipe on page 6.)

Gingerbread Puppets

Have students reenact the story of *The Gingerbread Boy* to practice their speaking skills. Allow each student to choose his favorite character and provide the appropriate patterns (see pages 15 and 16) for him to color and cut out to make a paper-bag puppet. Provide each child with a white or brown paper bag. Assemble the puppets as shown and allow time to reenact the story. Each time the story is retold, encourage the students to chime in with the words that their puppets would say.

Gingerbread Boy Pattern
Use with "Save The Gingerbread Boy!" on page 7, "The Gingerbread Boy Search" on page 8, and "A Gem Of A Gingerbread Man" on page 9.

Gingerbread Graphing

Graph the pieces that were eaten first!

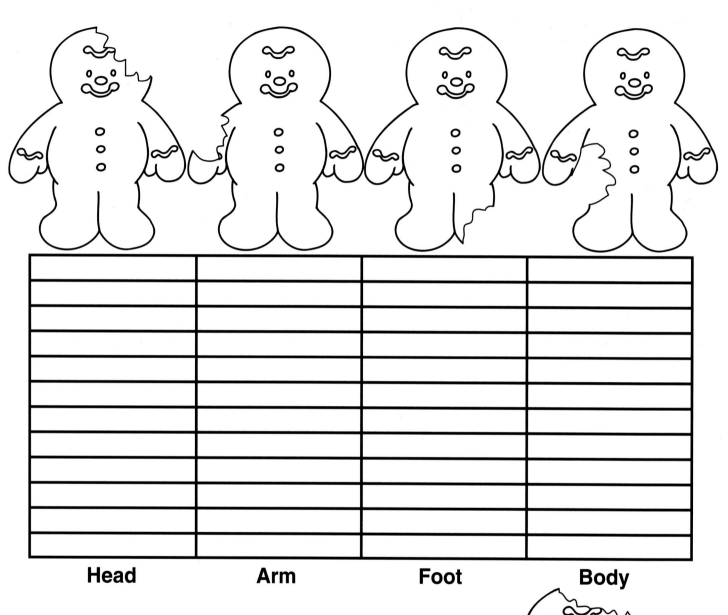

| **Head** | **Arm** | **Foot** | **Body** |

1. What part did you bite first?

2. Why did you choose that part?

3. What was the most popular part to be eaten first?

4. What was the least popular part to be eaten first?

5. Why do you think the results came out the way they did?

How Big Is The Gingerbread Boy?

Cover the Gingerbread Boy to find the *area*.
Outline the Gingerbread Boy to find the *perimeter*.
Record your answers on the grid.

How many?	Area	Perimeter
1. Mini marshmallows		
2. Cinnamon hearts		
3. Jelly beans		
4. Raisins		

- -

Note To The Teacher: Use with "Units Of Gingerbread Measurement" on page 9.

Down The Gingerbread Lane

Cut and paste the characters.
Trace the path.

1. The old woman's house is on West Gingerbread Lane.

2. The cow is in the barnyard.

3. The horse is in the north pasture.

4. The threshers are in the east field.

5. The mowers are at the south gate.

6. The gingerbread boy is east of the duck pond.

7. The fox is on the south side of the Little River.

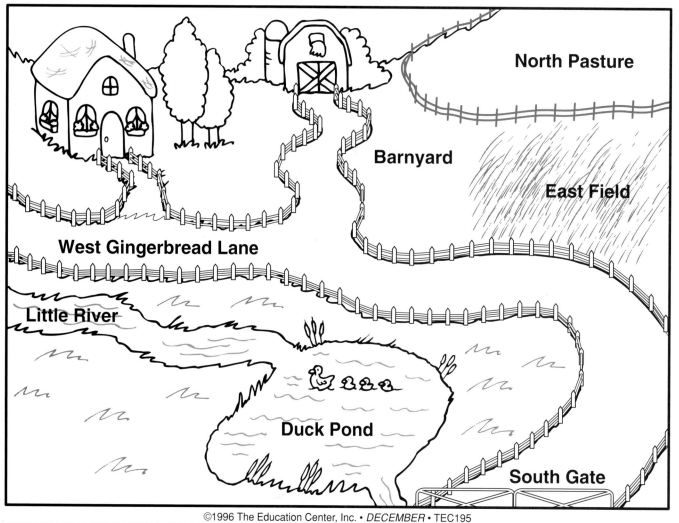

North Pasture

Barnyard

East Field

West Gingerbread Lane

Little River

Duck Pond

South Gate

Note To The Teacher: Use with "Down The Gingerbread Path" on page 8.

fox's tail

fox

horse

Patterns

Use with "Gingerbread Puppets" on page 10.

cow

old man

mower/
thresher

old woman

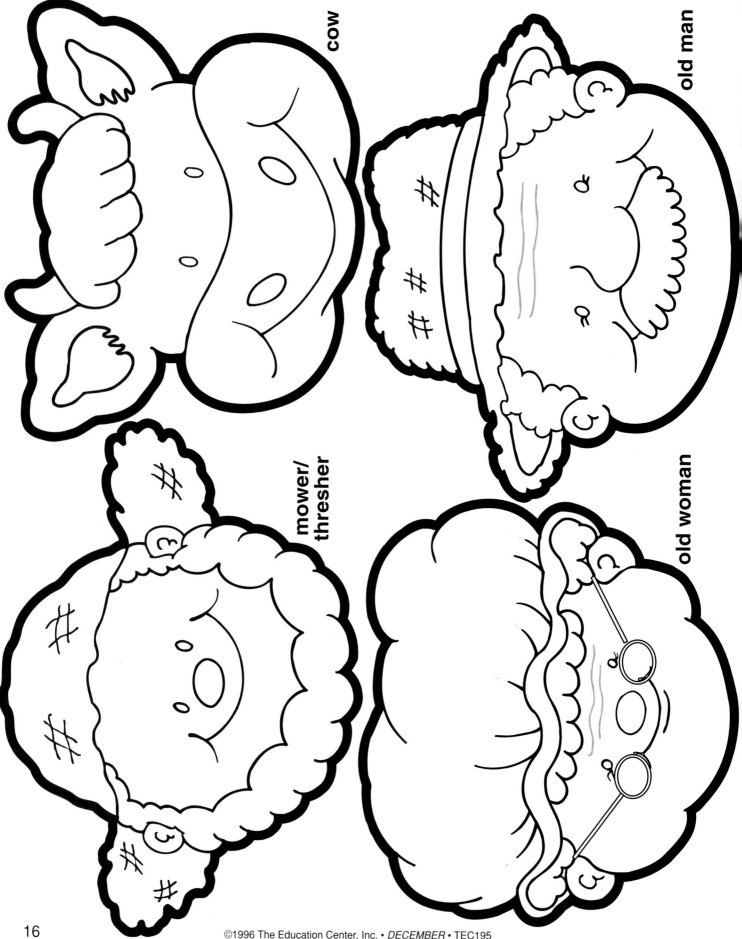

HANUKKAH LIGHTS

This Jewish festival of lights is celebrated for eight days by lighting candles, eating special foods, singing songs, playing games, and giving gifts to the children in Jewish families. The celebration begins at sundown each night, since the Hebrew calendar is based on the moon instead of the sun. Share in the history and traditions of Hanukkah with these activities that are sure to light up faces in your classroom.

ideas by Carolyn Kanoy and Kathy Wolf

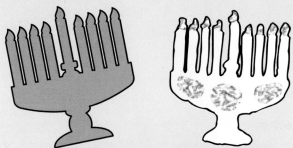

Making A Menorah

A very special candleholder is used each night of Hanukkah. It is called the *menorah*. There are varied designs and shapes of menorahs, but each shares common characteristics. All menorahs have a place for eight candles and the leader candle, called the *shamash*. The shamash stands taller than the other candles and is used to light each of the other candles. On the first night, the shamash is used to light one candle. One additional candle is lit each night until all eight candles are lit on the last night. A special blessing in Hebrew is recited when the menorah is lit each night.

If possible, have a Jewish person bring in a menorah and explain the symbolism of the eight candles. Duplicate a class supply of the reproducible on page 21 so each student can read about the history of Hanukkah. Then have each student make a menorah out of dough. Provide the pattern on page 22 for each child to trace and cut out a menorah from cardboard. Prepare salt dough by mixing 4 cups all-purpose flour, 1 cup salt, and 1 1/2 cups cold water. Give each child a portion of dough. Demonstrate how to mold the dough into the shape of a menorah cutout. Add candy sprinkles if desired, and allow the dough to dry.

Lots Of Latkes!

Potato pancakes, called *latkes*, are a favorite traditional food at Hanukkah. They are fried in oil—symbolic of the tiny amount of oil found in the temple. Help children prepare latkes following the recipe below. Then let them sample the mini latkes as you read *Latkes And Applesauce* by Fran Manushkin (Scholastic Inc., 1990). This story is about a family who grows their own potatoes and apples for their Hanukkah latkes and applesauce. One year a blizzard covers up their food. It looks like there will be no latkes and applesauce, but a stray dog and cat save the day.

To make mini latkes, peel and grate five medium potatoes. Grate one medium onion. Add 1/2 teaspoon salt and 1/4 teaspoon of pepper. Add one egg. Mix all together and add three tablespoons of flour or matzo meal. Drop spoonfuls of this mixture into very hot oil in a frying pan. Turn and cook until crisp on both sides. Drain on paper towels. Have children top their latkes with applesauce if desired.

Dreidel Days

A favorite Hanukkah game is played with a top called a *dreidel*. According to legend, the Jews used the dreidel game to trick the Syrian soldiers long ago. The Jews were forbidden to practice their religion and had to hide their holy books from the Syrian soldiers. If they heard soldiers approaching while they were studying, the Jewish boys would hide their scriptures and pull out a dreidel.

Today children enjoy playing the dreidel game with peanuts, pennies, nuts, or *gelt* (chocolate coins wrapped in gold foil). If the dreidel lands on the נ *(nun)*, the player gets nothing. If the dreidel lands on the ג *(gimmel)*, the player gets the pot. A ה *(hay)* signifies that the player gets half the pile and a ש *(shin)* means you add a piece to the pot. Each letter stands for the first letter in the four Hebrew words meaning "A great miracle happened there." The miracle, of course, occurred when the Maccabees recaptured their temple in Jerusalem, and the oil burned for eight days.

Have students play with a dreidel for math practice. Duplicate the pattern on page 23 on construction paper for each child to cut out and assemble. Have students print the numerals 6, 5, 4, and 3 on the dreidel instead of Hebrew letters. To play, pair students and provide peanuts in the shell. Each student in turn spins two times and adds (or multiplies) both numbers. Spin 6 + 6 or 3 x 4 to win instantly!

Light The Candles!

To culminate your study of Hanukkah, have students participate in choral speaking and candle making. Duplicate the rhyme on page 20 for each child. Divide the class into eight groups and assign verses to recite. Allow time to practice.

Then have each group create a candle to light during the choral speaking. Purchase the following materials from a craft store: paraffin wax, stearine crystals, wire wicking, and candle scents or colors, if desired. You will also need a hammer, a nail, newspapers, clean milk cartons, an old coffee pot or an empty three-pound coffee can, scissors, and a roll of duct tape. Cover your work area with newspaper and have pot holders handy.

Use the hammer to break the block of paraffin into smaller pieces. Place pieces of wax in the pot and heat on low heat until melted. Discuss the appearance of the wax before and during the heating. Introduce the words *solid* and *liquid*. Point out that scents and colors can be added to the wax in its liquid state. Allow students to add the crystals, a few drops of scent, and colors to the wax. (Tell students to use caution because the pot and wax are hot.)

Give each group a carton and a three-inch piece of wire wicking. Have one student in each group reinforce the carton by wrapping a length of duct tape around the middle. Another student uses a nail to poke a small hole in the center of the carton bottom, inserts the wick, and secures it by taping it on the bottom. Help the students pour two inches of the melted wax into each carton. Allow the candles to set overnight. Peel off the cartons to reveal the eight candles. Have a *shamash* (helper candle) and a lighter ready.

Now you're ready to invite another class for a choral presentation! Darken the room and have each group in turn recite its verse and light its candle with a shamash. Students will glow with pride as their candles burn brightly for a Hanukkah remembrance.

Hanukkah Reading To Light Up The Season

Toby Belfer Never Had A Christmas Tree

by Gloria Teles Pushker
(Pelican Publishing, 1991)

Growing up in the only Jewish family in a small town is not a problem for Toby Belfer. She has never had a Christmas tree, and she has never wondered why. She knows Jewish people don't celebrate Christmas, but she also enjoys helping her Christian friends decorate their trees. One year Toby invites her friends to share in her family's Hanukkah traditions. Toby's friends learn the story of the miracle that is remembered by the lighting of *menorahs*. Everyone has fun playing *dreidel* and winning *gelt*.

Read this book aloud and ask students how Toby might have felt as the only Jewish girl among friends who were looking forward to Christmas. Introduce the word *traditions.* Discuss the ways that students' families celebrate in December. Ask what Hanukkah traditions they learned from Toby's family.

To prepare for creative writing, write the following words on dreidel shapes: *applesauce, candles, dreidel, gelt, Hanukkah, Jewish, latkes, Maccabees, matzo meal, menorah, potatoes, prayers, shamash,* and *Torah.* Help students place the cutouts in alphabetical order. Then have each student use the words to write a letter to Toby Belfer telling what traditions he learned from her story.

The Chanukkah Guest

by Eric A. Kimmel
(Holiday House, Inc.; 1988)

Children will delight and giggle at the little old grandmother who can't see well enough to tell that the bear at her Hanukkah dinner isn't the rabbi that she invited. After reading ask students to tell what might happen if the nearsighted grandma had opened her door to The Big Bad Wolf, The Seven Dwarfs, or Goldilocks.

Then have each student rewrite the tale, adding another incredible guest at the Hanukkah dinner table! Have each child choose a storybook character, sports star, or other unlikely guest to show up at Grandma's house for Chanukkah. Have students write stories and draw the tracks left by their surprise guests. Share the stories and make a list of all the guests. Bind the stories along with the guest list into a class book titled "More Chanukkah Guests."

Hanukkah!

by Roni Schotter
(The Trumpet Club, 1990)

The latkes have landed and a Hanukkah feast begins! Your students will love the rhymes and illustrations that show how one family celebrates Hanukkah. Read this book aloud and ask students to name the ways that this family prepares for Hanukkah. Reread the book, having youngsters chime in with the rhyming words. Have students illustrate favorite lines from the story. "Potato pancakes in the air. Latkes flying everywhere!"

Eight Candles Burning Bright

Candle 1   The time has come.
            We've waited all year.
            It's finally sundown
            And Hanukkah is here!

Candle 2   There are presents to open
            And so much to do.
            There are prayers to recite
            On night number two.

Candle 3   We're standing very proudly,
            Our flames burning bright.
            Our lights stand for hope
            On this, the third night.

Candle 4   The children play with dreidels
            In a circle on the floor.
            They try to win the gelt.
            It's night number four!

Candle 5   On the fifth night of Hanukkah,
            Songs fill the room.
            Voices are singing
            A very familiar tune.

Candle 6   Latkes are cooking;
            In oil they will fry.
            It's hard to believe
            Six nights have gone by.

Candle 7   Lots of presents
            Are wrapped in blue.
            On this seventh night of Hanukkah,
            They may be for you.

Candle 8   We're all burning proudly.
            The eighth night is here.
            We'll put away the menorah
            Until this time next year!

                                —Carolyn Kanoy

©1996 The Education Center, Inc. • DECEMBER • TEC195

20 **Note To The Teacher:** Use with "Light The Candles!" on page 18.

A Miracle Happened There!

At Hanukkah, we remember a **miracle**. It happened more than 2,000 years ago. The king of Syria named **Antiochus** tried to make everyone pray to Greek gods. The Jewish people wanted to worship their one God. The king's army attacked the Jewish holy place. They took the holy things from the **temple**. They put Greek **idols** in the temple instead.

A small group of Jews led by **Judah Maccabee** fought bravely against the Syrian soldiers. Finally the Maccabees won. They had to clean up their temple. They had to find oil for the holy light that always burns in the temple. The Jews found a small amount of oil. But it was only enough to burn for one day. Then a miracle happened—the oil burned for eight days!

Today Jewish people celebrate Hanukkah by lighting eight candles in a holder called a **menorah**. The menorah has eight candles plus a helper candle called a **shamash**. The shamash is used to light the other candles. Hanukkah is also called the **Festival of Lights** because the candles shine brightly for eight nights.

Draw lines to match the words to the meanings.

1. shamash   pray to, honor
2. worship   helper candle
3. temple   fighters, army
4. soldiers   holy place, church
5. miracle   the leader of a small band of Jews
6. idol   the Syrian king
7. menorah   a statue, a god
8. Hanukkah   a wonderful event, a blessing
9. Antiochus   Festival of Lights
10. Judah Maccabee   a special candleholder

Menorah Pattern
Use with "Making A Menorah" on page 17.

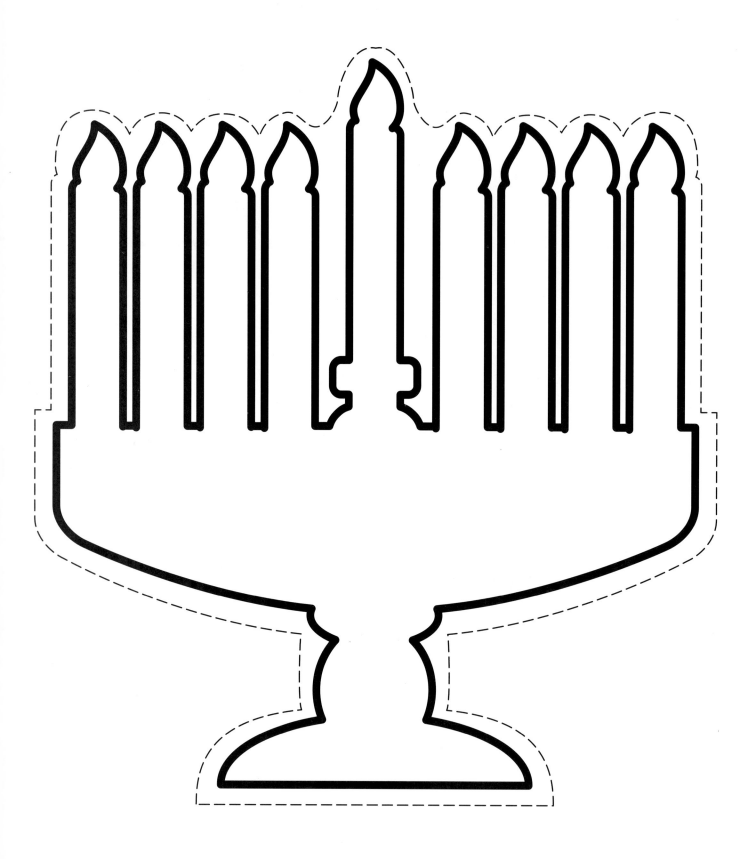

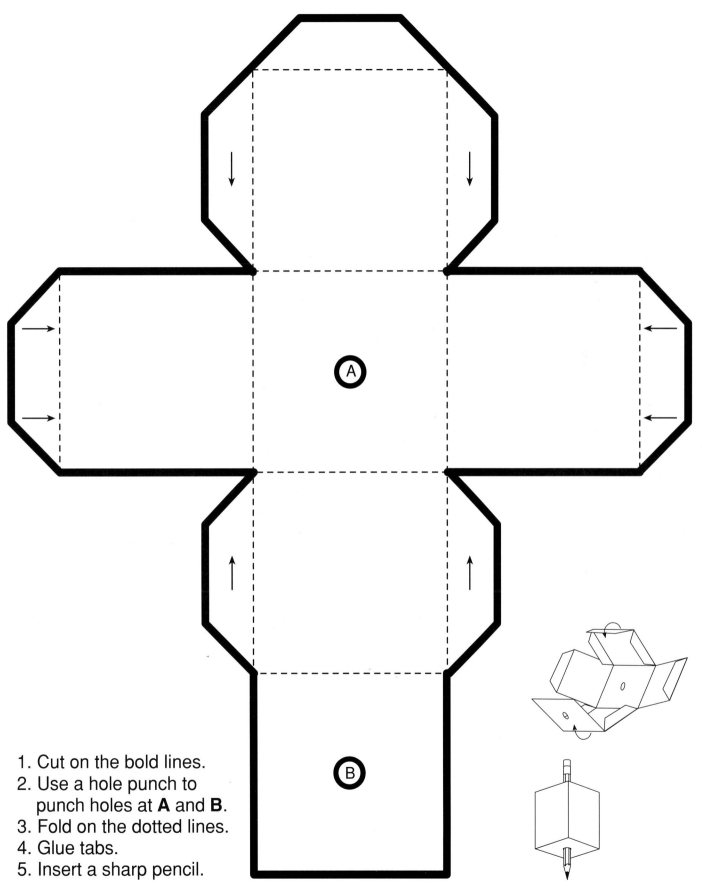

1. Cut on the bold lines.
2. Use a hole punch to punch holes at **A** and **B**.
3. Fold on the dotted lines.
4. Glue tabs.
5. Insert a sharp pencil.

Bravo For Jan Brett!

Use this collection of activities to introduce students to the fabulous fairy tales and folklore of Jan Brett.

ideas by Resa Audet

Behind The Scenes With Jan Brett

Jan Brett spent a great deal of time as a child retreating into the pages of her beautiful picture books. There were moments when she felt like she became a part of the fictional world that she was reading about. Brett's dream was to write and illustrate books that held this same kind of magic for other children. Her dream came true when her first original work, *Fritz And The Beautiful Horses,* was published in 1981. Since then Jan Brett has combined her love of Old World folklore and her interest in foreign art and architecture to create a treasured collection of books.

Warm Up To Reading With Jan Brett!

This hands-on display will build interest in Jan Brett's charming picture books. Have each child cut out a mitten from a 12" x 18" sheet of white construction paper. Instruct the child to illustrate the front of the mitten with a scene from her favorite Jan Brett book, then label the illustration with the book title. Ask each child to write a summary of the story on a sheet of paper, leaving out the ending so as not to spoil it for someone else who has not read the book. Staple each mitten onto a bulletin board as shown; then slip the matching summary sheet inside the mitten. Add a border of colorful construction-paper mittens (see page 28) and the title "Warm Up To Reading With Jan Brett!" Encourage students to reach into the mittens to learn more about Jan Brett's marvelous masterpieces. Duplicate the reproducible bookmark on page 28 for each student to list the books he has read.

Annie And The Wild Animals

(Houghton Mifflin Company, 1990)

Annie is lonely after her cat Taffy disappears, so she leaves corn cakes in the snow to lure a new pet. Little does she know that a great many wild animals, big and small, will be attracted by the smell of her delicious corn cakes! After reading this story, ask students why so many animals wanted Annie's corn cakes. Explain that food is scarce in the winter; then tell students that they can help some animals find food this winter by making bird feeders.

Each child will need a large pinecone, peanut butter, cornmeal, birdseed, a plastic knife, and twine. First reduce the sticky feel of the peanut butter by mixing it with a small amount of cornmeal. Have each child spread the peanut butter mixture on the pinecone; then help him coat the peanut butter with birdseed. Hang the bird feeders from the low branches of trees using twine. What a "tweet" way for youngsters to help their fine, feathered friends.

The Mitten

(The Putnam Publishing Group, 1990)

Read aloud this wonderfully funny story about a boy, a lost mitten, and a host of forest animals that decide to make the mitten into a home. As you read the story, point out the clues in the borders that help the students predict upcoming events. As students look at Baba's expression on the last page, ask them if they think that Nicki or Baba will ever solve the mystery of the stretched mitten.

Then add a fun twist to your story session by inviting students to solve the "Mystery In The Mitten." Gather a large mitten and a variety of objects that will fit inside the mitten. Out of view of students, place an object in the mitten. Challenge a student to guess what is in the mitten. Tell the student that he can gather clues by shaking the mitten, smelling the mitten, and touching the outside of the mitten with his fingers. If he guesses correctly, let him place the next object in the mitten. This activity is bound to be a hit. After all, everybody loves a mystery!

Goldilocks And The Three Bears

(Sandcastle Books, 1990)

The three bears have gone for a walk while their porridge cools. When Goldilocks arrives at the bears' empty house, she decides to go in and have a peek. Curiosity brings unexpected results, however, in Jan Brett's charming version of this classic tale.

After reading aloud this story, treat each youngster to a bowl of porridge that's just right. Prepare a large pot of oatmeal (or use individual, unflavored packets of instant oatmeal); then provide spoons, bowls, and toppings such as honey, brown sugar, granola, fresh or dried fruit, and cinnamon and other spices for students. As their porridge cools, invite groups of students to act out the story of *Goldilocks And The Three Bears*. Grrreat fun!

Christmas Trolls

(The Putnam Publishing Group, 1993)

How does Treva help two mischievous trolls celebrate their first Christmas? Find out by reading aloud this story; then make troll pencil toppers inspired by Brett's cute characters. Each child will need one copy of page 28, fake-fur scraps, crayons, scissors, glue, and a pencil. To make a pencil topper a child cuts out the pattern along the solid lines; then she folds the pattern in half along the dotted lines. The child colors each side of the pattern and glues on fur scraps to make hair. Glue the edges of the pattern together as shown. The child slips the pencil topper over the eraser end of her pencil. These terrific trolls are tops!

1. Fold.

2. Decorate.

3. Place on pencil.

The Twelve Days Of Christmas

(The Putnam Publishing Group, 1990)

Tune into creative writing with this beautiful rendition of a beloved Christmas carol. After reading or singing this story aloud, divide your class into small groups. Provide each group with a booklet filled with six 12" x 18" sheets of drawing paper. Have each group cooperatively write the text for a new version of *The Twelve Days Of Christmas;* then ask the group members to illustrate each page and design a front cover for the book. Invite each group to share its story aloud with the class; then present these Yuletide treasures to the school librarian or principal.

On the first day of Christmas My true love gave to me

My own sweet, baby pony.

More Books By Jan Brett

Armadillo Rodeo (G. P. Putnam's Sons, 1995)

The Wild Christmas Reindeer (Scholastic Inc., 1990)

Fritz And The Beautiful Horses (Houghton Mifflin Company, 1981)

Town Mouse, Country Mouse (G. P. Putnam's Sons, 1994)

Beauty And The Beast (Clarion Books, 1990)

Berlioz The Bear (Scholastic Inc., 1991)

Pattern

Use with "Christmas Trolls" on page 26.

Mitten Pattern

Use with "Warm Up To Reading With Jan Brett" on page 24.

Bookmark

Use with "Warm Up To Reading With Jan Brett" on page 24.

Jan Brett's Books I Have Read:

Name

A Christmas World Tour

Pack your bags and grab your passports. Take off on a whirlwind holiday tour to learn about Christmas customs around the world. Your world travelers will be visiting six countries: Sweden, England, France, Germany, Italy, and Mexico.

ideas by Karen Ciampa and Kathy Wolf

Hop On Board The Holiday Express!

For a lesson in geography, have students trace their world travels on a holiday bulletin board. Cover your board with blue background paper. Enlarge, color, and cut out the airplane pattern on page 30. If desired, glue students' school photos to the airplane windows. Cut out several clouds from white paper. Mount the airplane, clouds, and title along with a world map. Duplicate six copies of the suitcase pattern on page 30 on brown construction paper to cut out. Label and number each of these six suitcase cutouts with one of the countries above. Have students locate their destinations and pin the suitcases to the map. Bon voyage!

Plan Your Travel Itinerary

To prepare for each stop on your Christmas tour, duplicate the world map on page 31 for each student. Ask students what they already know about each country on the itinerary. List their responses on a chart. On another chart list some things students would like to find out about each country. When you introduce each new country, have the students color that stop on their maps and map keys. Students may keep small travel diaries or journals in which they write facts about each country.

Apply For Your Passports

Explain to students that obtaining a passport is one of the first steps in planning any international travel. Travelers must present their passports for identification to enter each foreign country. Provide each student with a copy of the passport application on page 32. Help students fill in the blanks. After the applications are complete, provide a copy of page 33 for each student to fold into a passport booklet. Have each child complete the information and affix a photocopy of his school photo to his passport.

As you complete the study of Christmas in a country, allow each student to get his passport stamped. Assign a "passport agent" to affix a colorful Christmas sticker in the appropriate box on each passport. At the end of the unit, your students will have six stamps in their passports to show they are world travelers!

Pack Your Bags!

Here's a clever way for students to keep their passports, travel maps, and travel diaries and journals handy. Then have him create a suitcase from a 9 1/2" x 12" brown file folder. Have each student cut out handles from tagboard, glue them to the insides of the folder, and staple the two sides of the folder closed. Add details with a black marker, as shown. Laminate the suitcases for durability if desired. Provide an airline address label for each child to fill out and attach to his suitcase.

Have students place their passports, maps, and journals inside and hang their suitcases on the bulletin board for easy access. After they have visited each country, your tourists may decorate their suitcases with symbols of the country or with Christmas stickers.

Airplane Pattern
Use with "Hop On Board The Holiday Express!" on page 29.

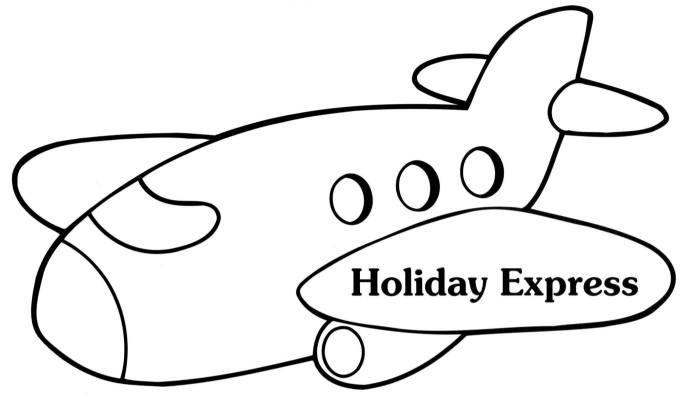

Suitcase Pattern
Use with "Hop On Board The Holiday Express!" on page 29.

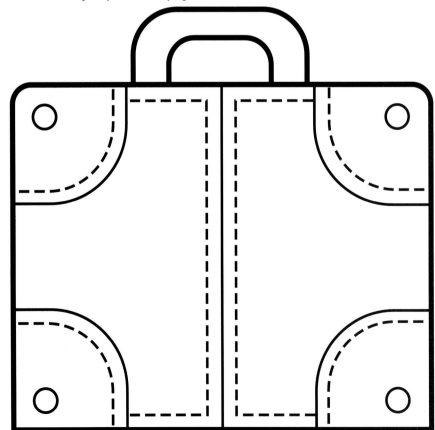

Christmas-Around-The-World Map

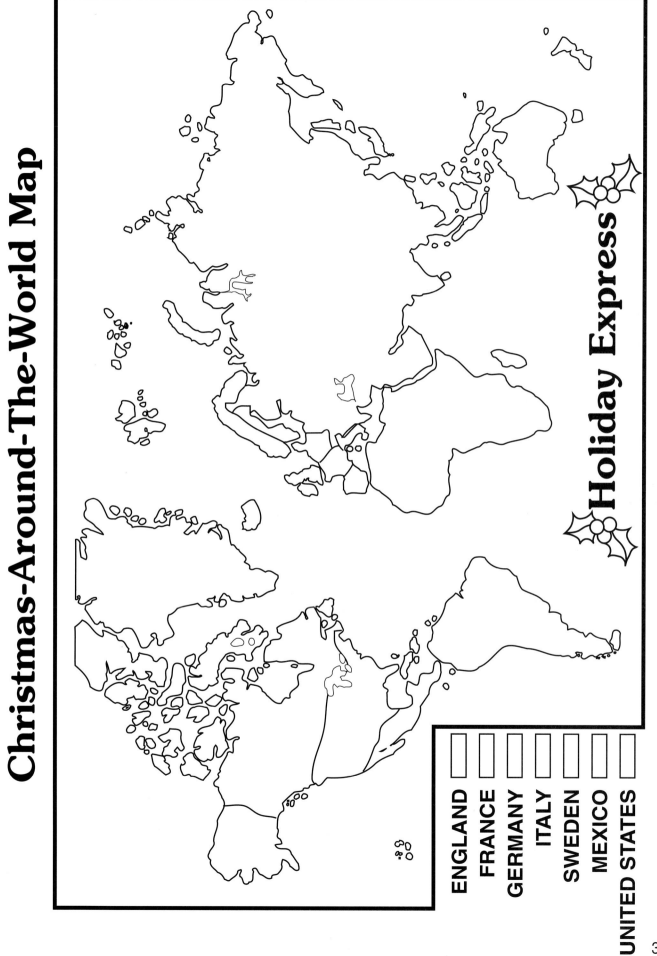

Holiday Express

ENGLAND
FRANCE
GERMANY
ITALY
SWEDEN
MEXICO
UNITED STATES

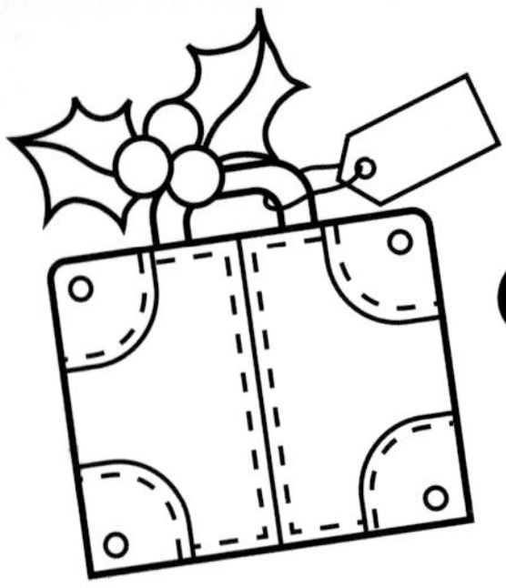

Passport Application
Christmas Around The World

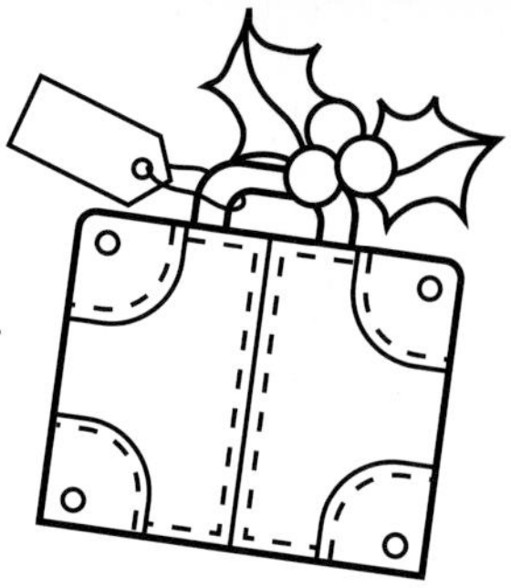

Last name ____________________

First name ____________________

Street address ____________________

City ____________________ State ____________________

Date of birth ____________________

Place of birth ____________________

Height ____________________ Weight ____________________

Color of hair ____________________ Color of eyes ____________________

Citizen of what country? ____________________

Signature ____________________ Date ____________________

Passport Approved

☐ yes ☐ no

Glue photo here.

Official Seal

 Note To The Teacher: Use with "Apply For Your Passports" on page 29.

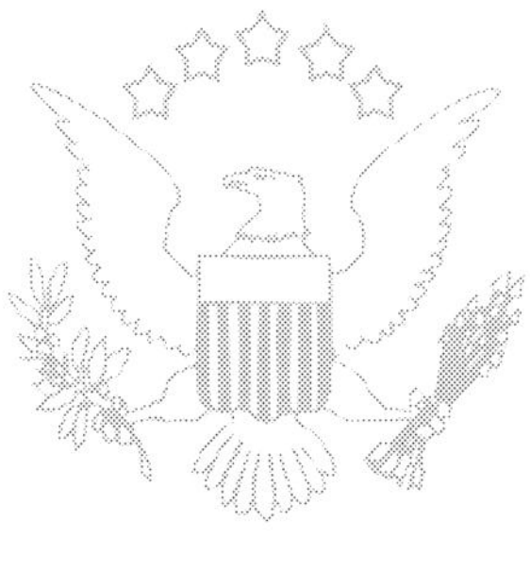

HOLIDAY EXPRESS PASSPORT TO THE WORLD

Fold here.

This passport certifies that the bearer is a citizen of the world. The bearer is entitled to travel and enjoy, but must always learn and respect the cultures of others.

Glue your photograph here.

Fold here.

Name _____

School _____

Birth Date _____

Hair Color _____

Eye Color _____

ITALY	SWEDEN
PLACE STAMP HERE.	PLACE STAMP HERE.
ENGLAND	**MEXICO**
PLACE STAMP HERE.	PLACE STAMP HERE.
GERMANY	**FRANCE**
PLACE STAMP HERE.	PLACE STAMP HERE.

Welcome To Merry Olde England

Have students arrive in England to the sounds of recorded Christmas carols as you serve warm, spiced apple cider from a large punch bowl. Play "Deck The Halls"; "God Rest You Merry, Gentlemen"; "Wassail Song"; and "We Wish You A Merry Christmas." Printed words and music for all of these can be found in *Tomie dePaola's Book Of Christmas Carols* (G. P. Putnam's Sons, 1987). Then locate England on the world map. Explain that England, Wales, and Scotland make up Great Britain. On Christmas Day, many British families tune in to hear the queen give a Christmas message on the *tellie.*

Explain that caroling is one of our Christmas customs that originated in England. On the days before Christmas, carolers go from house to house singing joyful songs. The singers are invited inside to partake of a warm fruit punch or *wassail* from a large wooden bowl. *Wassail* comes from the old Anglo-Saxon greeting *waes hael* and translates as "what hail" or "here's to your health!"

Father Christmas

Sending Christmas cards is another tradition that began in England. The first cards, similar to postcards, were printed in the 1840s. By the 1870s, the custom had spread throughout Britain. To encourage critical thinking, display Christmas cards with pictures of Father Christmas and Santa Claus. Have students compare the two characters. *(English children hang their stockings by the fireplace for Father Christmas who—wearing a red suit and hat like our Santa Claus—delivers gifts to children.)* Then have students create original Christmas cards showing Santa. Allow students to exchange cards with classmates. Ho, ho, ho! It's jolly good fun!

Celebrate Boxing Day

December 26 is a national holiday in England called *Boxing Day*. Long ago on this day, noblemen gave boxes of gifts to their servants. Today collection boxes in churches are opened and the contributions are distributed to the poor. Explain this English tradition and have students decorate a collection box for donations for a needy family. Encourage students to bring in canned foods or contribute change, if possible, to buy a fruit basket or frozen turkey.

Create A Christmas Cornucopia

Christmas trees in English homes often include cornucopia ornaments to symbolize the spirit of sharing the plenty with others. Have students make miniature cornucopias to decorate their family Christmas trees. Duplicate the pattern below on colored construction paper for each child to cut out. Have each child form a cone and staple or glue it together. Have students decorate their cornucopias with ribbon, sequins, glitter, stickers, and lace or rickrack. Attach a piece of gold cord to each cornucopia, as shown, for hanging. Fill the cornucopias with wrapped Christmas candies, and allow students to take them home.

Cornucopia Pattern
Use with "Create a Christmas Cornucopia."

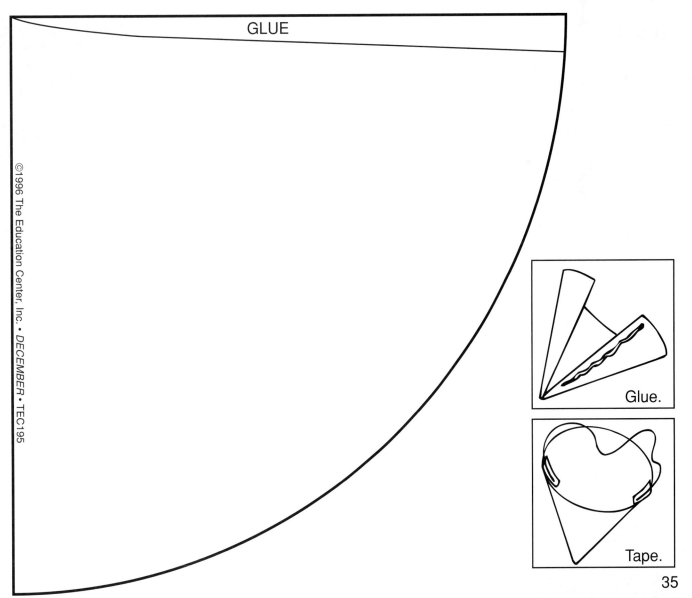

GLUE

Glue.

Tape.

Bring In A Büche De Noël

On Christmas Eve, many French families attend midnight Mass and then have a festive, late-night supper called a *réveillon.* To create the atmosphere of a French Christmas, darken the classroom, light several candles, and serve the traditional French dessert called *büche de Noël,* or Christmas log. This cake roll is frosted to look like a yummy Yule log—a large piece of tree trunk. In ancient times, people thought an unburned Yule log had magical powers. Today people burn Yule logs to bring good luck.

Play recorded versions of the traditional French carols "The First Noël" and "Bring A Torch, Jeannette, Isabelle!" For printed words and music, see pages 10 and 60 of *Tomie dePaola's Book Of Christmas Carols* (G. P. Putnam's Sons, 1987). Explain that these traditional French Christmas songs are hundreds of years old. Print the following vocabulary words on individual cards and ask students to match the French to the English words: l'enfant—the baby, un flambeau—a torch, la mère—the mother, belle—beautiful, beau—handsome. Locate France on the tour map and have students color it on their maps. Don't forget to stamp their passports!

Joyeux Noël, Babar!

In France children put their shoes in front of the fireplace on Christmas Eve. Father Christmas, also known as *Père Noël,* fills the shoes with candies and nuts. Read aloud *Babar And Father Christmas* by Jean de Brunhoff (Random House, Inc.; 1968). In the story, Babar gets a magical red suit that enables him to fly so he can help Father Christmas deliver presents to the elephant children. After reading the book, discuss why this famous French elephant was looking for Father Christmas.

For creative-writing practice, have students "send" postcards showing Babar and his dog Duck looking for Father Christmas. Provide each student with a blank 5" x 7" index card and have him draw Babar on one side. Have each student write a message on the back telling where Babar is and address the postcard to his family. Provide Christmas stickers for students to use as stamps.

A Noël Welcome

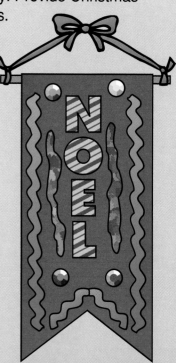

At Christmastime the French hang door decorations on their front doors to welcome friends and neighbors. Have your students create a Noël door hanger to take home. Each student will need a 12" x 5" piece of colored construction paper, a six-inch dowel, Christmas gift wrap, scissors, glue, sequins, rick-rack, ribbon, and glitter.

To make a hanger, cut a V at the bottom of the construction paper as shown. Fold the top edge over and glue it in place to form a casing for the dowel. Trace the word *NOEL* on wrapping paper. Cut out the letters and glue them vertically on the construction-paper banner. Decorate the banner with sequins, glitter, and rickrack. Insert the dowel and tie a piece of ribbon to each end. Help each student tie the ribbon in a bow. Allow students to take their banners home.

Oh, Tannenbaum!

To introduce your study of German customs, read *An Early American Christmas* by Tomie dePaola (Holiday House, Inc.; 1987). Discuss how the tradition of the lighted Christmas tree came to America from Germany. The trees once were decorated with lighted candles, paper roses, cookies, and fruit. Today glass ornaments, straw stars, little gingerbread men, hand-carved wooden angels, and tinsel are common.

Locate Germany on the world map. Then have students help you decorate a small Christmas tree in your classroom. Invite a craftsperson to demonstrate the art of German paper cutting called *scherenschnitte* (SHEAR-en-scnhit-tah). Provide templates (available at craft stores) for students to trace and then cut out ornaments from white paper. As you decorate the tree together, play the song "Oh, Tannenbaum" ("Oh, Christmas Tree"). See page 66 of *Tomie dePaola's Book Of Christmas Carols* (G. P. Putnam's Sons, 1987) for the words and music.

Have your "passport agent" affix a Christmas-tree sticker to each passport to represent Germany and say, *"Fröhliche Weihnachten!"* (FROY-likh-eh vy-NAHCK-tehn), which means "Merry Christmas!"

More Horsepower For St. Nick

St. Nicholas was a beloved Christian bishop who died long ago in the AD 300s. He is remembered for his kindness to children. On December 5, the eve of St. Nicholas Day, St. Nick brings gifts to children in parts of Germany. Children fill their shoes with straw and carrots for St. Nick's horse and place their shoes beside the fireplace. In return St. Nick leaves candy and presents for the children. Sometimes St. Nicholas may have his assistant *Kris Kringle* deliver the gifts. In other parts of Germany, *Christkindl*, the Christ Child, sends *Weihnachtsmann* (Christmas Man) with gifts for the children on Christmas Day.

For critical-thinking practice, ask students to compare St. Nick and Christmas Man to Santa Claus. Discuss the need for more horsepower for St. Nick. Then have students write letters to St. Nick telling why they think he should trade in his horse for eight reindeer and a magic sleigh. Or have each student design an even faster means of transportation for Santa and include an illustration with his letter. Share their letters before mailing. What's faster than a speeding bullet? A supersonic Santamobile!

Buon Natale!

In Italy, Christmas is a religious and family holiday. Before Christmas a *presepio,* or nativity scene, is set up in every church and in many homes. Some families gather at the manger scene to say prayers each evening of the nine days before Christmas. Distant family members travel home for the holidays. On Christmas Day, families go to church together.

Before Christmas small groups of musicians from the mountains of the Abruzzi region travel from town to town. These fellows, called *zampognari,* look like shepherds in traditional sheepskin jackets and laced sandals with pointed toes. The zampognari go from house to house playing hymns on their bagpipes.

If possible share a nativity scene with your class and discuss the role of the shepherds. Read *The Little Drummer Boy* by Ezra Jack Keats (Aladdin Paperbhacks, 1987) and provide musical instruments for students to perform.

Introducing La Befana

Italian children may receive gifts from *Babbo Natale,* the Italian version of our Santa Claus, on Christmas morning. Traditional gift giving comes 12 days later on Epiphany, January 6, when families remember the journey of the Three Wise Men to Bethlehem to present gifts to the *Bambino Gesù.*

Italian legend has it that the three kings rested on their way to Bethlehem at the home of an old woman. They asked her to join them in bringing gifts to the Baby Jesus, but the old woman said she was too busy sweeping her house. Later she reconsidered but lost her way. To this day she is looking for the Christ Child. *La Befana,* the kind old witch whose name derives from *Epiphania,* flies on a broomstick through windows and down chimneys. She fills the shoes of good children with toys and candy. Bad children receive pieces of coal!

Read *The Legend Of Old Befana* by Tomie dePaola (Harcourt Brace & Company, 1980); then have students model a story about La Befana. Duplicate a copy of the reproducible on page 39 for each student to complete. Then help each child decorate a broom like La Befana's. Purchase a small broom for each child (these are available at craft stores). Each child makes a gift card, punches a hole in it, and ties it with a red ribbon as shown. Tell students to take their brooms home to grace their holiday hearths.

A Taste Of Italy

On Christmas Eve, Italians fast from sunset on December 23 to sunset on December 24. Traditionally for Christmas Eve dinner, fish or baked eel is served. On Christmas Day, an Italian feast may include pasta, roast turkey or veal, fish, vegetables, cheeses, and pastries. A traditional loaf-shaped Christmas cake made with raisins and citron called *panettone* is given as a gift to the hostess—much like fruitcakes are given as gifts in America.

Italian chefs are famous for gracing holiday tables with delicious filled pastries called *cannolis.* Provide these Italian pastries for students to sample. Or have your little bambinos prepare some. Purchase pastry shells and the ingredients for instant vanilla pudding. Have students help you prepare the pudding following the directions on the box. Fill a pastry bag with the pudding and allow each student to fill his shell. Buon!

ITALY

LA BEFANA IS SPECIAL IN ITALY

La Befana is a special person in Italy.

Shall I tell you why?

Because _____

Because _____

Because _____

Because _____

Just because—that's why!

La Befana is a special person in Italy.

Note To The Teacher: Use with "Introducing La Befana" on page 38.

Say Hello To Saint Lucia!

Welcome your students to your classroom dressed as Saint Lucia. Introduce yourself and explain that Lucia's lighted crown reminds us that the long, winter nights will soon be replaced with days of longer sunlight. Help students locate Sweden on your world travel map. Point out its proximity to the North Pole.

Explain that in Sweden the Christmas season begins with St. Lucia Day, December 13. On that morning, the oldest daughter—or the mother if there is no daughter—dresses as Saint Lucia in a white dress with a red sash and wears a crown of greenery with seven lighted candles. She awakens the family and serves coffee and sweet buns to family members in their beds.

Have students create St. Lucia crowns of paper to wear. Duplicate the pattern on page 41 on white construction paper for each child to color and cut out. Provide a strip of green construction paper for each child, and have him glue on his candles as shown. Fit and staple each strip to make a headband. Have both boys and girls wear their crowns as you serve a snack of sweet buns and warm cocoa.

Meet A Swedish Christmas Elf

Swedish families give gifts wrapped in paper and sealed with wax. Gift tags are attached with riddles or verses giving hints to what is inside. The gifts are put in a wicker basket and distributed on Christmas Eve. In addition, a gnomelike gift-giver called *Jultomten* or *Tomten* leaves gifts for the children. Children in Swedish farm families believe that these beneficent gnomes live in their barns. Read aloud *The Christmas Tomten* by Viktor Rydberg (Coward, McCann & Geoghegan, Inc.; 1981). After reading, ask students what they would say to the tomten if they discovered him.

To encourage creative writing, have students discover a gift-wrapped box from the Christmas tomten. Use the pattern on page 41 to make a Christmas gnome cutout or purchase a gnome doll, and place it in a gift-wrapped box. Write a riddle on the gift tag, as shown. Place the box where students will find it. Have students read the riddle and guess the contents; then open the box to reveal the gnome cutout or doll.

Next have each student create a gift for the Christmas gnome and write a corresponding riddle. Provide each student with a 9" x 12" piece of construction paper, a 9" x 6" piece of gift wrap, ribbon, a paper scrap, and a duplicated copy of the gift tag on page 41. The student writes his riddle on the gift tag and cuts it out. He folds the construction paper in half and draws his gift inside. To complete the project, the student glues the wrapping paper and a ribbon to the front to resemble a present and attaches his gift tag. Display the mystery packages on a bulletin board. Allow students to read the riddles and lift the flaps to find the answers.

SWEDEN

40

Christmas Gnome Pattern
Use with "Meet A Swedish Christmas Elf" on page 40.

©1996 The Education Center, Inc. • *DECEMBER* • TEC195

Gift Tag Pattern
Use with "Meet A Swedish Christmas Elf" on page 40.

WHAT'S INSIDE?

I am _____ and _____

I sound _____

I feel _____

You find me in (on, at) _____

_____

Can you guess what I am?

©1996 The Education Center, Inc. • *DECEMBER* • TEC195

Pattern
Use with "Say Hello To Saint Lucia!" on page 40.

©1996 The Education Center, Inc. • *DECEMBER* • TEC195

41

Feliz Navidad!

Welcome students to Mexico with a display of real poinsettias. Explain that Dr. Joel Roberts Poinsett, the American ambassador to Mexico from 1825 to 1829, introduced this plant to the United States. The poinsettia is also known as *flor de la noche buena,* or the "flower of the holy night." Have students examine a poinsettia more closely. Point out that the red, pink, yellowish, or white petals are really *bracts,* or special leaves that surround the actual tiny flowers. Caution students that, if eaten, the leaves and stem of the poinsettia can cause a severe stomachache. In addition the plant's sap can irritate the skin and eyes.

Read *The Legend Of The Poinsettia* retold and illustrated by Tomie dePaola (G. P. Putnam's Sons, 1994). Then have students make a beautiful basket of paper poinsettias to decorate your classroom bulletin board. To make a ten-inch, pinwheel-shaped bloom, each child will need the following:

— a ten-inch square of red bulletin-board paper
— a small square of yellow construction paper
— pieces of green bulletin-board paper for leaves
— glue, scissors, and a hole puncher

Demonstrate how to make a paper poinsettia and have students follow along as they make their own flowers.

1. Fold the square in half diagonally and crease.
2. Open and repeat the folding from the other corners.
3. Cut on each fold about three-fourths of the way toward the center.
4. Glue each corner to the center of the pinwheel.
5. When all four corners are glued, cut and glue a small yellow circle to the center.
6. Glue two red leaves and two green leaves to the back of each pinwheel.

To make a bulletin-board display, cut a large basket from brown paper, adding woven details with a black marker. Staple the ten-inch poinsettias close together as shown and add the title "Feliz Navidad."

To make individual poinsettia ornaments, provide each child with a five-inch square of red bulletin-board paper to make a paper poinsettia as above. Provide him with a piece of gold cord to glue to the back. Students can hang these bright ornaments on their family Christmas trees as remembrances of your trip to Mexico.

MEXICO

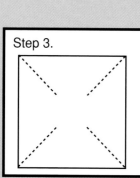

Step 3.

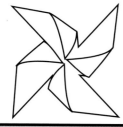

Step 4.

Las Posadas And Piñatas

The nine days before Christmas are called *Las Posadas* in Mexico. Each evening beginning on December 16, processions make their way through the village streets to reenact the journey of Joseph and Mary to Bethlehem. The travelers, led by a boy and girl carrying figures of Joseph and Mary, go from house to house looking for *posada,* or shelter, each night until Christmas Eve. Each posada is followed by a feast at a participant's home where the children try to break a papier-mâché, candy-filled container called a *piñata.* Read *Pancho's Piñata* by Stefan Czernecki and Timothy Rhodes (Hyperion Paperbacks For Children, 1994) and discuss this old Mexican legend of the Christmas Star. If possible hang a piñata for students to break open.

For a lesson in geometry and following directions, provide templates and colored paper. Have each student cut out one four-inch circle and five triangles. Have the student assemble the pieces as shown and glue them onto a 9" x 12" piece of blue construction paper. Next provide small squares of colored tissue paper for the student to glue onto his star shape to resemble a piñata. Have him add foil star stickers as shown. Hang these piñata pictures on a line strung across the room.

KWANZAA

Kwanzaa is an African-American holiday celebrated for seven days each year from December 26 to January 1. Kwanzaa is not a religious holiday. It was created in 1966 by Dr. Maulana Karenga to promote awareness of traditional African customs and family values. It is a time for people of African descent to celebrate their kinship and evaluate their lives.

ideas by Pam Kucks

The Seven Principles Of Kwanzaa

NGUZO SABA (en-GOO-zoh SAH-bah)

The seven-day celebration is centered around seven Kwanzaa principles. On each day of Kwanzaa, a candle is lit to highlight one of the seven principles. Share these principles with your class by writing the words and definitions on a chart. Add a geometric border of red, green, and black—the colors for the holiday.

- UMOJA—(oo-MO-jah)—*Unity.* We help each other.
- KUJICHAGULIA—(koo-jee-cha-goo-LEE-ah)—*Self-determination.* We decide things for ourselves.
- UJIMA—(oo-JEE-mah)—*Collective work and responsibility.* We work together to make life better.
- UJAMMA—(oo-jah-MAH)—*Cooperative economics.* We support our community.
- NIA—(NEE-ah)—*Purpose.* We have a reason for living.
- KUUMBA—(koo-OOM-bah)—*Creativity.* We make things with our minds and hands.
- IMANI—(ee-MAH-nee)—*Faith.* We believe in ourselves, our forefathers, and the future.

For each day of the celebration, teach the meaning of a principle with an activity:

1. Gather your students to set the mood for a day of unity. Have the class sing a favorite song or recite a special poem together in the morning.
2. To practice self-determination, have students vote on a free-time activity.
3. To demonstrate collective responsibility, provide a task that requires cooperation to complete. Divide the class into groups. Send each group on a scavenger hunt to find Kwanzaa-related items such as a straw mat *(mkeka),* ears of corn *(muhindi),* or fruits and vegetables *(mazao).*
4. To encourage awareness of community, provide telephone books and have students look in the Yellow Pages™ for local businesses. Have each student list one for each of the following categories: a movie theater, a restaurant, a grocery store, a doctor.
5. To emphasize that each person has a purpose, have each student write down on an index card what he would like to accomplish that day. At the end of the day, have students pull out their cards for self-evaluation. Allow each student who determines he has accomplished his goal to choose a sticker to affix to his card.
6. To motivate creativity, provide materials at a center so each student can create a Kwanzaa bracelet or necklace by stringing red, green, and black beads in a unique pattern. Allow students to wear their creations as reminders of Kwanzaa.
7. To emphasize faith in the future, have each child think of a career or job he or she aspires to; then have each student draw a picture of himself in this role.

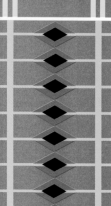

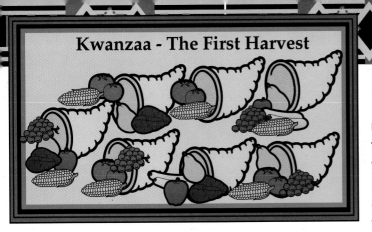

Kwanzaa - The First Harvest

First Fruits

The word *Kwanzaa* comes from Swahili, an East African language. It is derived from *kwanza,* which means "the first." (The extra *a* gives the holiday name seven letters—one for each of the seven Kwanzaa values.) The phrase *Matunda ya kwanza* means the "first fruits," referring to the yearly harvest. To create a bulletin-board display for the celebration of Kwanzaa, have students make cornucopias.

Enlarge and duplicate the cornucopia pattern on page 48 on brown construction paper for each student. Have each student cut out his cornucopia. Next distribute colored tissue or construction paper from which students can cut out fruits and vegetables. (See patterns on page 48). After students have glued the fruits and vegetables to their cornucopias, collect the cornucopias and mount them on a bulletin board as shown. Add the title "Kwanzaa—The First Harvest." To create a border, use 1 1/2-inch strips of red, green, and black paper as shown.

To reap the rewards of this colorful display, ask students to bring in real fruits to make a Friendship Fruit Salad. Younger students can select, identify, and wash the fruits. Help older students peel and cut the fruits into bite-size pieces. Have each student sample one piece of each fruit before mixing the fruits together. Discuss why fruits are good for us and create a graph to show students' favorites.

Mkeka Mats

The *mkeka* (em-KAY-kah) is a mat, usually made of straw, displayed on the family's table at Kwanzaa time. Have your students weave African tradition into their school day by creating their own mkekas. Provide each student with three sheets of 12" x 18" construction paper in the three colors that represent the holiday: red, green, and black. Cut 1 1/2" x 12" strips for weaving from two of the three colors. Each student will need ten strips in all. Let each student use the third sheet to be the background color of his mat.

To prepare the background mat for weaving, fold the paper in half. Next, using a paper cutter, make long, vertical slits starting at the fold of the paper and ending at least one inch from the edge of the paper to prevent tearing. (Make the slits about 1 1/2 inches apart, leaving one inch from the top and bottom of the paper.) The students then weave in an over-under pattern, alternating the two colored strips. Secure each woven strip with a glue stick. When weaving has been completed, have students make small cuts along the sides of their mats to look like fringe. Have the students use their woven creations at snacktime.

Dance To The Beat

One of the seven principles of Kwanzaa, *Kuumba* (koo-OOM-bah), means "creativity." Part of the celebration on the day observing this principle involves music and dance. Invite students who play musical instruments to share their talents at an African Dance Festival.

To prepare, look in a local library or ask the music teacher for a collection of African dance music or folksongs on album or cassette. Play the music for the class and have the students listen for different instruments. Play the music again and have them move to the music.

As a culminating activity for the festival, obtain a bongo-type drum, some shakers, and some wood blocks from the high-school music department. Have the class stand in a circle. Select a few students to stand in the middle of the circle and play these instruments along with the recorded music while their classmates move around them. Alternate so every student gets a chance to play an instrument. This is one movement activity that just can't be beat!

Children Count!

At each Kwanzaa table one ear of corn, or *muhindi,* is placed on the mkeka mat to represent each child in the family. Create a class chart to show the number of ears of corn each family would need for its mat. Duplicate the corn patterns on page 49 for each child. Have the student cut out the number of ears of corn he needs to represent the number of children in his family. Then have each student attach the ears of corn to the chart in a column. Have students compare, add, and subtract using the information on the chart. Challenge the students to make up word problems using the chart.

A Gift Of Love

Handmade gifts, or *zawadi* (zah-WAH-dee), are given to family members on the sixth night of Kwanzaa. Allow each student to make a special necklace to show love for a family member. Provide ziti- or rigatoni-type noodles and red and green tempera paint. Have students paint the noodles red and green. Allow the noodles to dry overnight. Have each student cut two 2-inch circles from black tagboard. With a large hole puncher, make a hole in each circle as shown. Give each student a 24-inch piece of black yarn. The student threads the noodles, alternating colors and adding the black circles. Help each student tie his necklace and wrap the gift in red and green tissue paper. Tie the packages with black ribbon or yarn. Encourage students to present the zawadi at a family gathering.

Seven Candles For Kwanzaa

by Andera Davis Pinkney
(Dial Books For Young Readers, 1993)

This colorful book about Kwanzaa helps to explain the weeklong celebration. It highlights the African words used during the holiday and gives the phonetic spellings. The detailed pictures show the family preparing for each day of the celebration.

After reading, have your students brainstorm a list of family-related activities. Next have each student draw a picture of his family doing one of the activities listed. Label each picture with each family's name. Put all the pages together in a book. Give the book a colorful cover with a geometric border. In the center, write the word "FAMILY" with a black marker and add a red paper heart on each side of the word. Put the book on display at the reading center in your classroom for everyone to enjoy.

My First Kwanzaa Book

by Deborah M. Newton Chocolate
(Scholastic Inc., 1992)

This story of the Kwanzaa celebration is told by a young boy. He celebrates this African-American holiday with his family and learns about his heritage. The author takes the reader through the holiday one day at a time. Brightly colored pictures help to explain what is happening on each day. When reading the story aloud, point out the *kinara* (kee-NAH-rah) pictured at the bottom right-hand corner of each page. Explain that a kinara is a candleholder usually made of wood. Each night of Kwanzaa, one candle is lit and the principle for that day is discussed.

Have students light a large bulletin-board *kinara.* Enlarge, color, and cut out the pattern on page 49. (The center candle is black, the three candles to the left are red, and the three to the right are green.) Mount the kinara on the bulletin board. To "light" the candles use either orange chalk or construction paper to make little "flames." The black candle is the first lit; then on each following day, alternate lighting the red and green candles until all seven are lit on the final day.

Each morning, have one student light the appropriate candle and another student say, *"Habari gani"* (hah-bar-ee gah-nee)—the Kwanzaa greeting that asks, "What is the news?" The answer given by the whole group should be the principle for the day. Lead the class in a discussion on the principle for that day.

Patterns
Use with "First Fruits" on page 45.

Corn Patterns
Use with "Children Count!" on page 46.

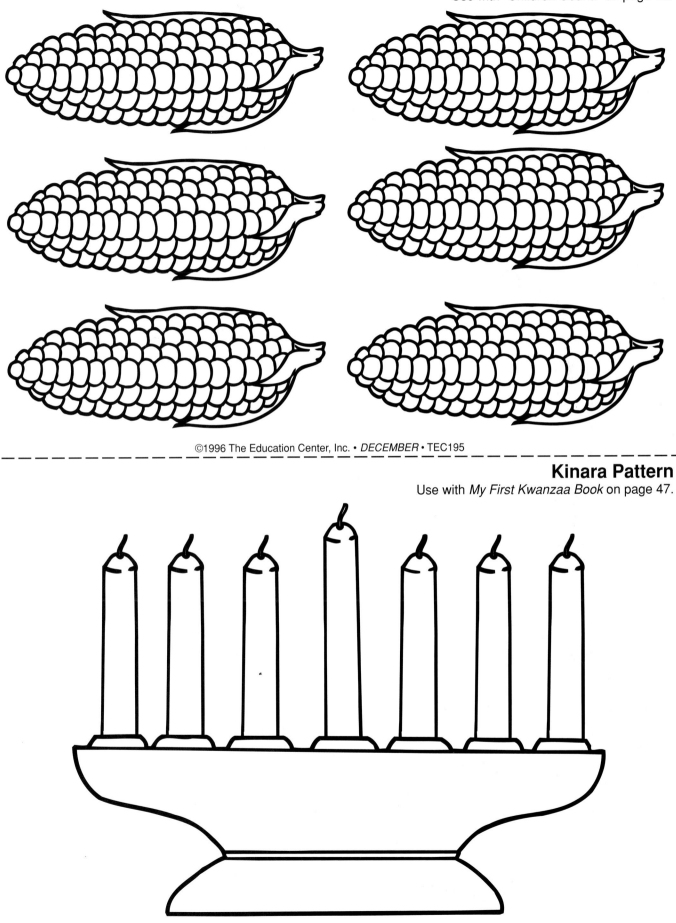

Kinara Pattern
Use with *My First Kwanzaa Book* on page 47.

Step aboard a classroom starship for a galactic voyage to the planets and beyond!
ideas by Susie Kapaun and Jan Masengale

Lost In The Solar System

Share *The Magic School Bus™ Lost In The Solar System* by Joanna Cole (Scholastic Inc., 1990). As a group, list all the places The Magic School Bus™ ventured in the solar system. Then let each student choose a planet in our solar system that he would like to explore. Have students do research on their planets and write on chart paper interesting facts that they find out about their planets. Display the charts on your walls.

Then, for creative writing, have each student write a story about his galactic travels and illustrate it. Remind each student to tell what means of transportation he used to reach his destination, what he discovered there, and what happened when he got lost on his way back to Earth. Allow students to share their adventures; then bind them together into a class book titled "Starship's Log From The Crew Of Room #_____."

Silly Solar-System Sentences

Give your students a reason to come up with silly sentences—the sillier, the better! Create mnemonic sentences as a way of remembering the planets in order. Share this example with your students: "My Very Excellent Mother Just Served Us Nine Pizzas!" Once students understand the concept of a mnemonic sentence, challenge them to make up their own silly sentences to help them recall the planets in order. (A dictionary makes a great resource for anyone who is at a loss for words.)

Then challenge your students to sequence the planets. First have each child cut a sheet of 12" x 18" black construction paper lengthwise, then tape the two pieces end to end to create a strip that is 6" x 36". Duplicate page 61 for each youngster. Have each student color, cut out, and glue the sun to the left edge of the strip, then color, cut out, and glue the planets in the sequence in which they orbit the sun. Those mnemonic sentences should come in handy for this astronomical activity.

Papier-Mâché Planets With Less Mess

Transform your room into a planetarium with student-created papier-mâché models of each planet and the sun. This technique can be done in less time and with less mess than the traditional method. The models will have a glossy sheen and do not require painting of the dried papier-mâché.

To prepare, obtain a variety of colors of bulletin-board paper as indicated below. Have students tear the colored paper into small pieces and put the pieces into one box for each planet and one for the sun:

Sun—red, orange, and yellow
Mercury—red
Venus—purple
Earth—blue and green
Mars—orange
Jupiter—brown, tan, red, and white
Saturn—yellow
Uranus—green and light blue
Neptune—light blue
Pluto—gray or black

Divide your class into ten groups. Select one group to create the sun. Then assign each of the other groups a planet to create. Give each group a balloon that has been inflated in proportion to its planet's size. Jupiter is the largest planet, followed by Saturn, Uranus, Neptune, Earth, Venus, Mars, Mercury, and Pluto. Provide an inflatable punchball for the sun (it makes a bigger sphere than a balloon).

Display pictures for students to use as references for the appearance of each of these heavenly bodies. Then mix two parts white glue with one part water. Using 1- to 1 1/2-inch brushes (one brush per group), have one member of each group brush glue on the group's balloon, and have the other group members apply torn-paper pieces to the balloon—one piece at a time—to resemble the surface of the planet or the sun. Keep the tied end of each balloon free to hang the completed project. Then have each group brush its balloon thoroughly with another coat of glue. (The key to success is to have all paper pieces wet and flat. Generally one layer of paper is sufficient, but a second layer will make the project more durable.) Set the models aside and allow them to dry overnight.

To create a model of the solar system, first hang the inflated punchball sun in the center of your room. Tie a desired length of string around the free end of each balloon and cut the string. Then hang the planets in the order in which they orbit the sun. Now there's a display that's out of this world!

Our Marvelous Moon

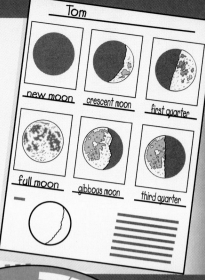

As the moon orbits Earth—which is about once every four weeks—it seems to grow larger and smaller. The moon actually remains the same. These apparent changes in the moon's shape depend on how much of its lighted side we can see.

Read aloud *The MOON Seems To Change* by Franklyn M. Branley (Harper Trophy, 1987). Help students learn the different phases of the moon and the terminology associated with these changes by completing the activity found on page 57. Have students apply these vocabulary words to the four main phases of the moon: *new moon, first quarter, full moon,* and *third quarter.* The following phases fall between the four main phases: *crescent moon* —between a new moon and a first quarter and again between a third quarter and a new moon; *gibbous moon*—between a first quarter and a full moon and again between a full moon and a third quarter.

Rocket Science

Want to travel to the moon? You'll need a rocket powerful enough to push your space vehicle out of Earth's atmosphere and away from the pull of gravity. Everyone in your class can be a rocket scientist with this science experiment that demonstrates *propulsion.* Each student will need a long balloon, tape, a drinking straw, a space-shuttle pattern, and scissors.

Duplicate the space-shuttle pattern on page 56 on white construction paper for each child to cut out. Then, using three pieces of tape, have students attach the straw as shown to the underside of the shuttle cutout.

Cut three lengths of string, each approximately ten feet long, and tie one end to the back of each of three chairs.

Divide your class into three groups and get ready for some friendly competition. With the help of a teammate, have one student from each team slide the loose end of a string through his straw. Next this student blows up his balloon and holds it, while his partner uses another piece of tape—sticky side out—to adhere his balloon to the straw as shown.

Now get ready to BLAST OFF! Have a member of each team pull its string tightly and, on the count of three, have students let go of the ends of their balloons. Watch the rockets go and record which team's rocket was the fastest! Once every student has had a chance to release his rocket, ask students why they think this experiment worked. Here's why:

When a balloon is inflated, the rubber expands. When the balloon is released, the air is forced out—thus propelling the rocket on the string forward. This experiment demonstrates Newton's Third Law of Motion: *for every action, there is an equal and opposite reaction.*

Our Sensational Solar System

Turn your students into aspiring astronomers by creating booklets filled with interesting facts about our solar system. To make the booklets, duplicate pages 58–60 for each student. Instruct students to cut the pages apart, put them in the correct sequence, and then staple their booklets together. Have students complete the pages. Explain to students that scientists believe that there is yet another planet, Planet X, beyond the nine we know. On the last page of this booklet, have students draw a picture of what they think Planet X might look like.

Out-Of-This-World Literature

Set up a space shuttle for some out-of-this-world reading. Obtain a large refrigerator box and cover it with white bulletin-board paper. Have students decorate the box with colored markers to look like a space shuttle. Provide pillows for comfort, a flashlight, and a basket of books about space and space travel. Allow your student astronauts to crawl inside the shuttle for some quiet galactic reading.

Call Me Ahnighito

by Pam Conrad
(A Laura Geringer Book, 1995)

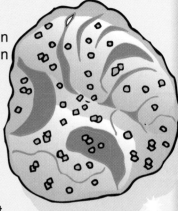

This story, told from a meteorite's perspective, describes how it was discovered in the Arctic and the long journey it made to the American Museum of Natural History in New York City. After sharing this story about a real meteorite with your youngsters, explain that a meteorite, made up of rock and metal, is a piece of a meteoroid that fell to Earth but was not completely destroyed upon entering Earth's atmosphere.

Then create your own meteorites for an imaginative art/writing activity. To begin, make a batch of salt dough using one cup of salt, one cup of flour, and 1/2 cup of warm water for each group of approximately five students. To achieve the gray rock look, add powdered, black tempera paint to the dough mixture. Divide the dough among the five students in each group. Allow each student to form his dough into a meteorite and sprinkle it with silver glitter for a metallic glow. After students have set their projects aside to dry overnight, have them follow up with this creative-writing activity. Ask each student to explain where he discovered his meteorite and how it got to be on display in your classroom. Allow students to label and share their discoveries on a table set up to look like a museum display.

Her Seven Brothers

by Paul Goble
(Bradbury Press, 1988)

Share this legend that explains how the Cheyenne believed the Big Dipper constellation was created. In the story, a young girl creates beautiful clothing for seven brothers whom she has not yet met. Upon finishing all seven outfits, the Indian girl sets out to find her seven brothers. Soon after finding them, a buffalo insists that the sister go with him to the chief of the Buffalo Nation. When the brothers refuse to give up their sister, the buffalo herd stampedes. In an attempt to escape, the youngest of the seven brothers shoots an arrow into the sky. It becomes a tall pine tree that the eight siblings climb. They climb so high that they become a permanent fixture in the night sky—the Big Dipper.

After sharing this exciting tale with your students, display pictures of other constellations, such as Orion the hunter and Canis Major, the greater dog. See *Stargazers* by Gail Gibbons (Holiday House, Inc.; 1992), which introduces students to constellations and telescopes. Discuss how ancient astronomers named these stars and explained the configurations. Then have students create their own original constellations and legends. To prepare, provide each student with a piece of black construction paper, Q-tips®, and a small container of white tempera paint. Have the student outline his constellation on black paper with pencil. Next have the student dip a Q-tip® into the paint and paint dots on his paper to represent the stars in his configuration. Have him name the constellation and label his drawing. While these art projects are drying, have each student write a legend about his constellation. After students share their tales, display the stellar projects for stargazing classmates.

A Trip To Mars

by Ruth Young
(Orchard Books, 1990)

This creative story begins as a young girl plans for her trip to Mars. The girl explains the steps that need to be taken in preparation for such a journey. Once she arrives, she shares some wonderful facts about the planet. After reading this delightful book to your youngsters, discuss what it would be like to be a space pioneer. Have each student design a spaceship in which he would travel should he decide to embark on such a trek. Then have him list the items he would want to take on board to survive. Allow pioneers to list two items *in addition to* their necessities.

Then have each student draw himself in a space helmet. Use the pattern on page 55 to make tagboard templates of the astronaut helmet. Have each student trace and cut out a helmet from white or gray construction paper. Students may decorate their helmets with flags and NASA symbols as shown. Have each student color an oval shape resembling his face, cut it out, and glue it behind the mask opening. Have each astronaut write a caption telling what he accomplished as a space pioneer, such as "First astronaut to take pictures of Pluto," "First astronaut to live in a space station for 50 years," or "First astronaut to blow bubble gum in space." Collect the helmets and captions, and display them on a bulletin board titled "The Astronauts' Hall Of Fame."

Earthlets As Explained By Professor Xargle

by Jeanne Willis
(Dutton Children's Books, 1989)

In his lecture on aliens, Professor Xargle describes the bizarre habits of earthlings. Students in his class learn the following: "Earthlets are born without fangs. At first, they drink only milk, through a hole in their faces called a mouth. When they finish the milk, they are patted and squeezed so they don't explode!" To learn about earthlings firsthand, the professor's students make some changes in their appearance and take a field trip to see *real* earthlings!

After reading the book, ask students if they believe that we have been visited by aliens, and have them explain why or why not. To follow up, have each student illustrate a "Marslet," a "Plutolet," a "Jupiterlet," or another appropriately named alien. Have each student list five things his alien does. To get them thinking creatively, ask students, "Do they drink mud through straws in their ears? Do they wear shoes on only five of their feet? Do they sleep standing on their heads?" After each student describes his alien, have the student design a spaceship his alien would use. Display students' aliens, spaceships, and lists.

(Other books about Professor Xargle and his students are *Earthmobiles As Explained By Professor Xargle, Earth Weather As Explained By Professor Xargle, Earth Tigerlets As Explained By Professor Xargle,* and *Relativity As Explained By Professor Xargle.*)

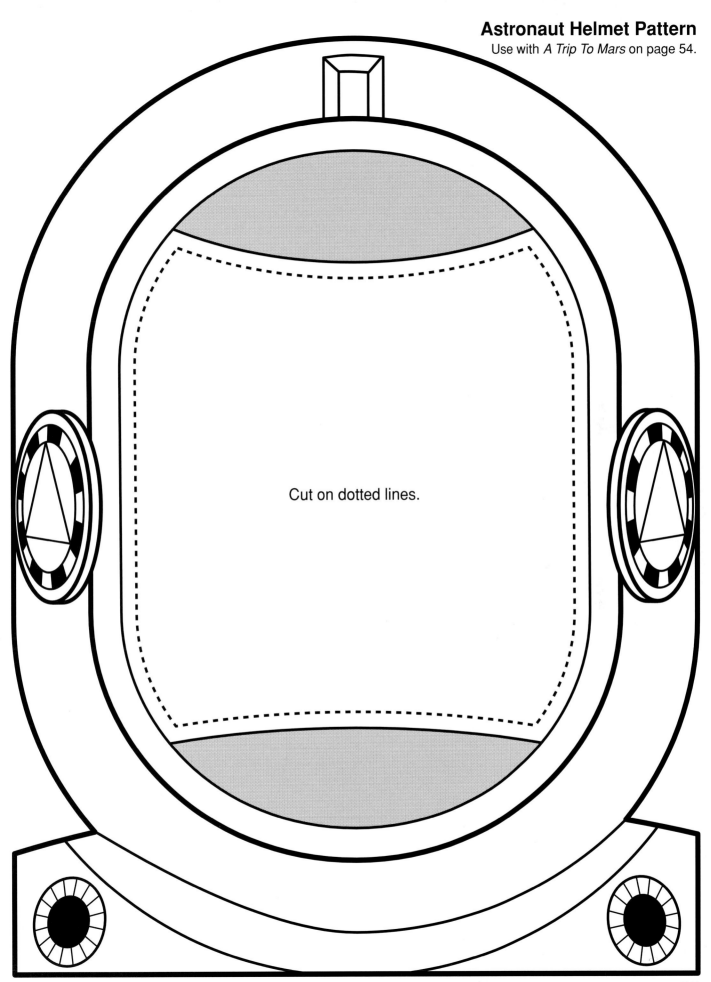

Cut on dotted lines.

Space-Shuttle Pattern

Use with "Rocket Science" on page 52.

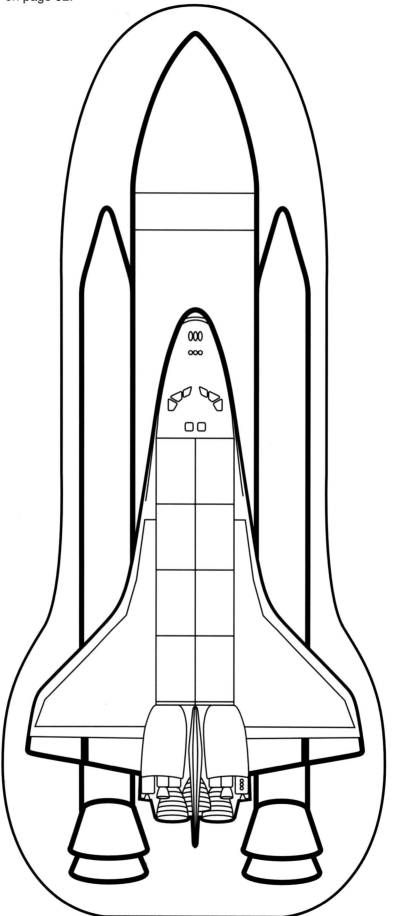

Name _____ *The moon*

Our Marvelous Moon

Label the different phases of the moon.

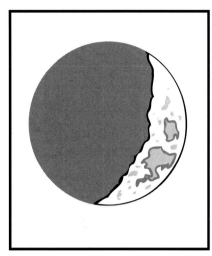
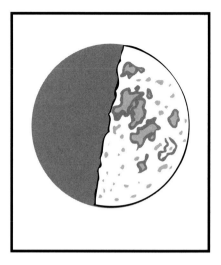

1. _____ 2. _____ 3. _____

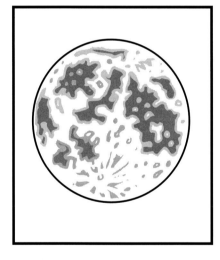
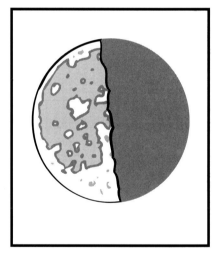

4. _____ 5. _____ 6. _____

Draw what the moon will look like next.

Word Bank:
new moon
crescent moon
full moon
first quarter
gibbous moon
third quarter

Bonus Box: Find out what kind of moon is in the sky tonight.

©1996 The Education Center, Inc. • *DECEMBER* • TEC195

Note To The Teacher: Use this page with "Our Marvelous Moon" on page 52. 57

Solar-System Fact Booklet Pages

Use these with "Our Sensational Solar System" on page 52.

The solar system is made up of meteoroids, comets, asteroids, more than 50 moons, and nine known planets that orbit the sun.

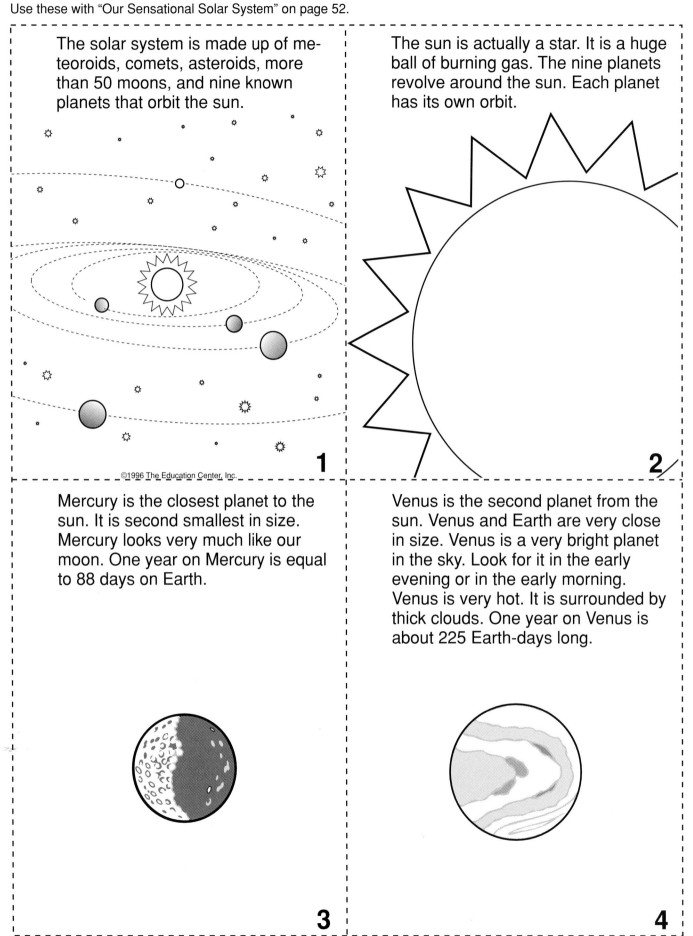

©1996 The Education Center, Inc.

1

The sun is actually a star. It is a huge ball of burning gas. The nine planets revolve around the sun. Each planet has its own orbit.

2

Mercury is the closest planet to the sun. It is second smallest in size. Mercury looks very much like our moon. One year on Mercury is equal to 88 days on Earth.

3

Venus is the second planet from the sun. Venus and Earth are very close in size. Venus is a very bright planet in the sky. Look for it in the early evening or in the early morning. Venus is very hot. It is surrounded by thick clouds. One year on Venus is about 225 Earth-days long.

4

Earth, the third planet from the sun, is our home. Earth is about 93 million miles from the sun. Earth has one moon. As far as we know, Earth is the only planet with plants and animals. One year on Earth is about 365 Earth-days. One day on Earth is 24 Earth-hours long.

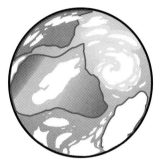

5

Mars is the fourth planet in our solar system. Mars has two moons. This planet is nicknamed "The Red Planet." It takes 687 Earth-days for Mars to go around the sun once. A day on Mars is 40 minutes longer than an Earth-day.

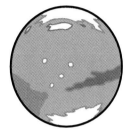

6

Jupiter is the fifth and largest planet. Jupiter has at least 16 moons. Jupiter has a bright red, stormy area called The Great Red Spot. One year on Jupiter is about 12 Earth-years long.

7

Saturn is the sixth farthest planet from the sun. It is very cold. Saturn has thousands of rings that are made up of ice, rocks, and dust. It also has at least 17 moons. It takes about 29 Earth-years to equal one year on Saturn.

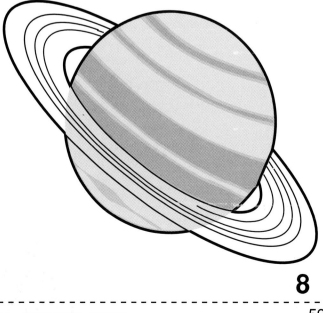

8

Solar-System Fact Booklet Pages

Use these with "Our Sensational Solar System" on page 52.

Uranus, the seventh planet, is tilted so that it is lying on its side. It rotates differently from all the other planets. Uranus is blue-green in color. It has at least 15 moons and 10 rings. One year on Uranus is as long as about 84 Earth-years.

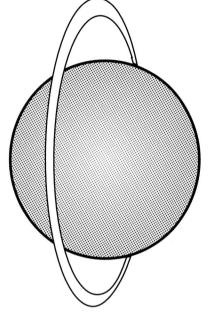

9

Pluto is the smallest planet. It is now the eighth planet from the sun. Pluto will only be the eighth planet until 1999 when Neptune and Pluto will cross orbits. Then Pluto will be the farthest planet from the sun for another 248 years.
Pluto's moon was discovered in 1978. One day on Pluto is six Earth-days long. It takes Pluto about 248 Earth-years to orbit the sun.

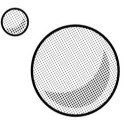

10

Neptune is the fourth-biggest planet. It is bright blue-green in color. Neptune has two moons, *Nereid* and *Triton.* Triton revolves around Neptune in the opposite direction of most other moons.
It takes Neptune about 165 Earth-years to orbit the sun. Neptune is now the ninth planet in our solar system. How old will you be when Neptune and Pluto switch places again in 1999?

11

Scientists believe there is yet another planet beyond the nine we know. Draw what you think Planet X looks like.

12

My Very Excellent Mother Just Served Us Nine Pizzas!

Color the sun and the planets.
Beginning with the sun, cut out and glue the sun and planets in the correct order.

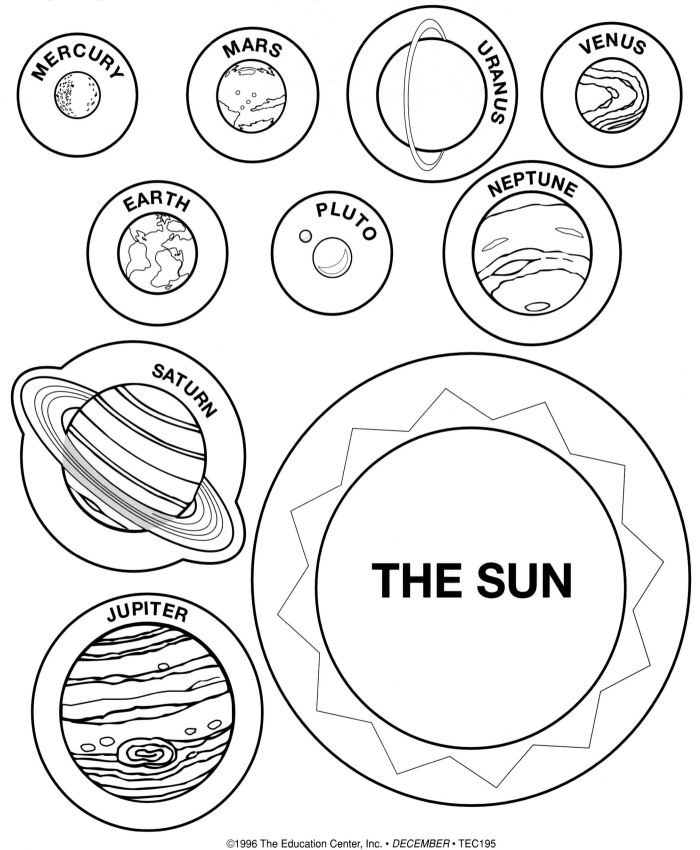

Teaching With TEDDY BEARS

No doubt each of your students has a "bear-y" special teddy bear! Use these cuddly best friends to introduce writing, math, and literature-based activities. Have students bring in bears during Teddy-Bear Week and plan a "jam-bear-ee" finale!

ideas by Susan Wilson, Jennifer Gibson, and Sharon Murphy

Teddy Bears Past And Present

Your students will enjoy learning how the teddy bear got its name. Tell students that in 1902 Teddy Roosevelt, the 26th president of the United States, went on a bear hunt. President Roosevelt refused to kill a bear cub that had wandered into his camp. The incident was portrayed in a newspaper cartoon with the caption "Teddy's Bear." Soon after, a shopkeeper began to sell cuddly toy bears called "Teddy's bears." Teddy bears remain a favorite toy of children today.

Tell your students that some people collect teddy bears as a hobby. Some of the earliest teddy bears ever made are very difficult to find and therefore are very expensive. Many of these antique teddy bears are dressed in outfits ranging from sailor suits to elaborate dresses. If possible, show pictures of antique teddy bears or ask a collector to share a display of teddy-bear memorabilia. Compare teddy bears of the past and present.

ABC Bears

Share the ABC name book, *Alphabears*, by Kathleen Hague (Holt, Rinehart and Winston, 1984). Together make a list of teddy-bear names from *A* to *Z*. Then make an alphabet quilt of teddy bears. Assign each child a teddy-bear name from *A* to *Z* and have him create an antique bear with that name. Give each student a copy of the patterns on page 76. Provide construction paper and/or fabric scraps for students to use to dress their bears in bathing suits, pajamas, sports outfits, tuxedos, etc. Then glue each completed bear on an 8" x 8" construction-paper square. Mount the finished quilt squares on butcher paper or on a bulletin board as shown to make a large quilt. Use a black marker to make stitches and hang the quilt for all to admire!

Teddy Tunes

Start each day of Teddy-Bear Week with rhythm and rhyme! Each morning teach a different poem or song that you have written on a chart. Try this teddy-bear song or the following traditional teddy-bear chant for starters.

I'm A Little Teddy Bear
(sung to the tune of "I'm A Little Teapot")
I'm a little teddy bear,
Soft and brown.
There's always fun
When I'm around!

I like to play all day
And cuddle at night.
If you get scared,
Just squeeze me tight!

Teddy Bear, Teddy Bear
Teddy Bear, Teddy Bear, turn around.
Teddy Bear, Teddy Bear, touch the ground.
Teddy Bear, Teddy Bear, reach up high.
Teddy Bear, Teddy Bear, touch the sky!

Teddy Bear, Teddy Bear, go upstairs.
Teddy Bear, Teddy Bear, say your prayers.
Teddy Bear, Teddy Bear, turn off the light.
Teddy Bear, Teddy Bear, say good night!

(The book *Bear Hugs* by Kathleen Hague [Henry Holt and Company, 1989] is a wonderful collection of teddy-bear poems that are perfect to share with students.)

Teddy-Bear Travels

To encourage journal writing, send a teddy-bear mascot around the school. Bring in a stuffed teddy bear and a suitcase to accompany it. Have your children vote on a name for the bear; then write a letter to introduce their Teddy to other classes. Tuck the letter in Teddy's suitcase along with a blank journal.

Then send Teddy on a trip around the school. Ask other classes to write new entries in Teddy's journal telling what he did in each classroom that day. As Teddy travels, children from each classroom fill up the pages in the journal. When Teddy has completed his travels, have your students take turns reading from the journal. Everyone will be surprised by your unexpected guest and what he learned at school!

Cassie

David

Stuffed Teddy Bears

To encourage descriptive writing, have students make stuffed bears. Ask each student to bring in one brown grocery bag. Enlarge the bear pattern on page 78 to make several tracing templates. Have each student trace a bear pattern twice on his bag and cut out both bears. Next, have each student glue wiggly eyes to the front of his bear and draw a nose and a mouth with markers. Help each student glue or staple the bears together—leaving the head area unglued. (Hot glue works best.) Each student stuffs his bear with crumpled tissue or newspaper. Finish gluing or stapling the bears together.

Use the patterns on page 78 for students to trace and cut out bow ties and tummy shapes from colored construction paper. Have each student name his bear, write his bear's name on the bow tie, and then glue the bow tie on his stuffed bear. Next have each student write a paragraph on the tummy shape that tells how his bear got its name. Glue the paragraphs to the bears' tummies as shown. Display the completed projects on a bulletin board with the title "Name That Bear!"

NAME THAT BEAR!

Casper

Teddy

Curly

Fold here.

Bears Of Many Colors

Create a border of multicultural bears. Cut white construction paper in half length-wise and give each child one piece. Have him fold his strip in half and then in half again as shown. On the chalkboard, demonstrate how to draw a bear on one side of the folded paper. (For younger students, prepare folded paper ahead of time and draw the pattern for them.) Then have each student cut on the lines. Remind him not to cut on the fold. When opened up, each student will have four teddy bears that are holding hands. Using markers or crayons, each student colors his bears and dresses them in outfits. Mount the bears on a good-work bulletin board with student papers.

Cinnamon Bears

These cinnamon bears add some spice to a poetry bulletin board! Give each student a copy of the bear pattern on page 77 to cut out. Have each student use this template to trace a bear shape on sandpaper and cut it out. Provide buttons for eyes and markers to draw noses and mouths. Have students glue the buttons on their bear cutouts. Then give each student a piece of piece of cinnamon stick to rub over her sand-paper teddy bear.

Next guide students in writing cinquains to describe their spicy bears. Model the process of creating a cinquain poem. The first and last lines are the same. Line two consists of two *-ing* words. Write three adjectives describing teddy bears on line three. Line four is a four-word sentence or phrase describing teddy bears. After students develop their cinquains, have them copy them over on small index cards. Each student then glues the index card on her bear's tummy. Display the bears and cinquains on a bulletin board with the title "Cinquains And Cinnamon Bears."

Teddy Bears
Cuddling, loving
Soft, furry, friendly
My very best friends!
Teddy Bears

Becky Gets
An A+
In Math!

News That Bears Repeating!

Here's a bulletin board that will make your students proud. Tell each child to color and cut out the teddy-bear and bow-tie patterns on page 76. Have each child also trace and cut out a newspaper rectangle and glue it to her bear's hands as shown. Display the bears on a bulletin board with the heading "News That Bears Repeating!" When a student reaches a goal, shows progress, or exhibits good behavior, use a black marker to write a headline on her bear's newspaper announcing her achievement. Duplicate the awards on page 75. Present one to each student when she achieves her goal or when she is "bear-y" well behaved. These words of praise will be as good as bear hugs for building self-esteem!

Teddy-Bear Squares

Introduce rhyming words with a game of "Teddy-Bear Squares!" Prepare a chart with four columns as shown. Use the pattern on page 77 to make four bear cutouts. Place a bear cutout at the top of each column. Program each cutout with one of the following letter combinations: *ear, air, are,* and *ere*.

Share the poem "Bears" by Ruth Krauss (available in the poetry book *Talking Tigers*, published by Mimosa Publications, 1995). Point out the words from the poem that rhyme with *bear* and ask students to think of more. As they offer suggestions, point out the various ways the vowel sound in *bear* can be spelled. List the words under the correct bear on the chart. After the chart is completed, hand out copies of the reproducible "Teddy-Bear Squares" on page 73. To make gameboards, have students fill in the squares using words from the chart. Provide Teddy Grahams® for students to use as markers.

To play, call out words randomly from the chart. Students cover their corresponding squares. A student calls out, "Bears!" when a row is covered horizontally, vertically, or diagonally. After several rounds of play, allow students to eat their teddy bears!

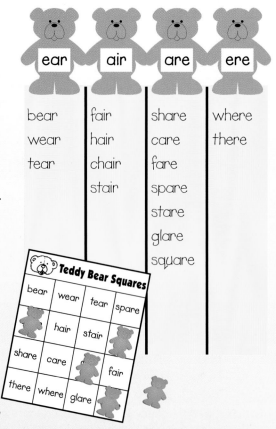

ear	air	are	ere
bear	fair	share	where
wear	hair	care	there
tear	chair	fare	
	stair	spare	
		stare	
		glare	
		square	

Teddy Phonics

Put teddy bears on parade for phonics. Duplicate the patterns on page 77 on light brown or yellow construction paper. Provide each student with a bear to cut out and label with a vowel sound. Then let the brainstorming begin! Have students write other words with the same sound and underline the vowel sound being studied. Hang the bears on a classroom clothesline or on the wall as a handy reminder.

Superteddy Tales

Your students will love writing about the one, the only, "Superteddy." Dress a stuffed teddy bear in a red cape and mask. Introduce your students to this teddy-bear hero. In a bear-shaped booklet, have each student write a heroic tale in which Superteddy saves the day.

To make a bear-shaped booklet, provide the pattern on page 77 for each student to trace and cut out two covers from brown paper. Have him trace his bear on top of several stacked sheets of lined paper and cut out all bear-shaped pages at once. Help each student staple his pages between the covers. Provide markers and colored construction paper for the student to use to decorate the front to look like Superteddy. After final drafts are written in the booklets, have students share their adventures of Superteddy with classmates and then take the booklets home to share with their families.

Teddy Bears' FAIR

Have a daylong Teddy Bears' Fair in your classroom! Devote one day during your thematic study to sharing teddy bears from home. Have students decorate the invitation on page 75 to take home to invite special bears to the fair. Notify parents with a letter and ask for donations of additional bears for students who are without teddies or for students who forget their bears. Choose from the following activities to make your fair a success:

- On the day of the fair, place several balloons around your class to set the mood.
- To help identify your "bear-y" special visitors, duplicate the reproducible nametag on page 75 on construction paper for each student to program with his bear's name. Have each student punch holes at both ends of the nametag and use yarn to tie the nametag around his teddy bear's neck.
- Sort and graph your bear visitors by different attributes. Use a floor graph, chart graph, or individual student graphs. Students can sort bears by colors, attire, or size.
- Reinforce ABC order with the following game. Form small groups of three or four students and have them arrange their teddy bears in ABC order using the names printed on the nametags. Then ask students to rearrange their bears, making groups of bears with names that begin with the same letter of the alphabet. For a finale, arrange all the bears in ABC order as a class.

Teddy Pretzels

See what good bakers you have in your class by making teddy-bear pretzels for snacktime. Have students help in measuring and mixing.

1 package yeast	1 egg, beaten
4 cups flour	1 tablespoon sugar
1 1/2 cups warm water	1 tablespoon salt

Mix together yeast, water, sugar, and salt. Stir in flour. Knead on table until dough is smooth. Shape dough into a teddy-bear shape. Brush with beaten egg. Sprinkle with salt. Bake in oven set at 425°F for 15 minutes or until browned.

Teddy Cakes

For an unforgettable ending to a special day, have a Teddy-Bear Tea. Serve teddy-bear tea (berry juice) and teddy cakes. To make a teddy cake, each child will need one cupcake, one mini-peppermint patty, two M&M's®, one Reese's® peanut-butter chip, a Twizzlers® stick (or licorice), a plastic knife, and chocolate frosting. Give each student an unfrosted cupcake. Let students frost their cupcakes. Give each student a peppermint patty and instruct him to cut the patty in half. To make the ears, attach the patties to the top of the cupcake with frosting as shown. Use M&M's® for eyes and a peanut-butter chip for a nose. Use clean scissors to cut small strips of Twizzlers® to form into a mouth. Let students eat their teddy cakes and tea with their teddy-bear guests as you read a book about bears! (See pages 71–72.)

The "Bear" Necessities For MATH

The Guessing Jar

Fill a jar with Gummy® Bears or Teddy Grahams® for estimation practice. Write the following rhyme on a bear cutout or on an index card and attach it to a teddy bear:
Look at all the bears in our jar! Can you guess how many there are?

Sit the teddy bear on a box near the jar. Place a pad of teddy-bear shaped notes and a pencil beside the box. Let each student write his name and his estimate on a note, then place it in the box. At the end of your unit, or during the Teddy Bears' Fair, count the Teddy Grahams® or Gummy® Bears together with your class. Count by ones, twos, threes, fives, tens, etc. Present the teddy bear to the student with the closest estimate and share the edible bears!

The Teddy Bears' Picnic

Give your students practice in problem solving. Share the cassette and book *The Teddy Bears' Picnic* by Jimmy Kennedy (Bedrock/Blackie, 1987) for some counting practice. Discuss the activities of the teddy bears; then give students copies of the reproducible on page 74. Provide Gummy® Bears or Teddy Grahams® for students to use as manipulatives.

Measuring Up With Teddy Bears

Here are some measurement activities that involve the students' own teddy bears. Have students bring their own teddy bears to school (or another stuffed animal if they don't have a teddy bear). Duplicate the reproducible on page 69 for each student. Pair students and have them work together to complete the charts about their bears.

- Help each student wrap string around his bear's belly. Cut the string and compare to see whose bear has the fattest tummy. Student pairs measure and record the length of the two strings.
- Demonstrate how to use a ruler or yardstick to measure the height of each bear. Student pairs record the two heights on their charts.
- Have your students determine the perimeter of each teddy bear. Have each pair place the smaller of the two bears on a table and use string to outline the bear. (If the string isn't staying in place, use tape to hold it in just a few spots.) Then have the students remove the string from the outline, measure it against a yard stick, and record the perimeter. Have them repeat the process with the larger bear.

When all pairs have completed their charts, share the results on a class chart. Let students discover who has the fattest, tallest, or shortest bears.

Measuring Up With Teddy Bears

Pair up with a buddy and measure your teddy bears.
Record and compare the results.

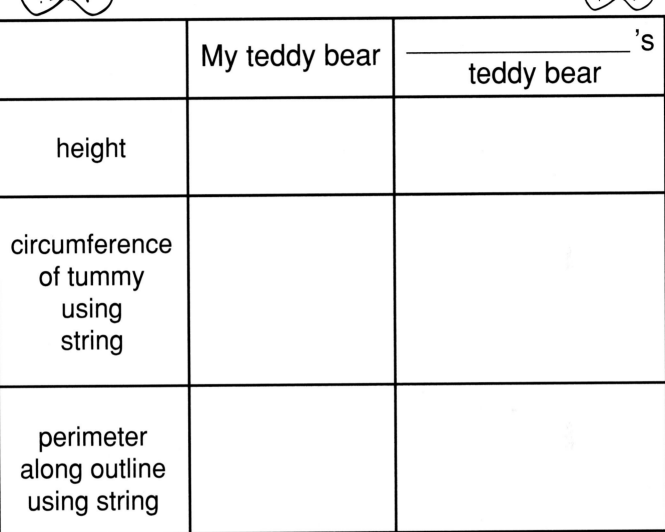

	My teddy bear	_____'s teddy bear
height		
circumference of tummy using string		
perimeter along outline using string		

1. The fatter bear measured _____.

2. The taller bear measured _____.

3. The shorter bear measured _____.

4. The perimeter of the smaller bear was _____.

Note To The Teacher: Use with "Measuring Up With Teddy Bears" on page 68.

Teddy Bears'
"JAM-BEAR-EE"

Culminate your study of teddy bears with a Teddy-Bear "Jam-bear-ee." Start your "jam-bear-ee" off by reading *Jamberry* by Bruce Degen. In this story a little boy and a bear go on a berry-picking adventure and have a "jam jam-boree." (Be sure to read the author's note at the end.)

After reading the book aloud, have your students name all the different kinds of berries they can think of. Then let them sample some different kinds of berries. Have some sour cream available for students to dip their berries in, just like the author did when he was little. (If you prefer, serve biscuits spread with different berry jams.) After the students have finished eating, do a graphing activity to see which type of berry was the most popular. During your Teddy-Bear "Jam-bear-ee," keep students and guests busy with the following activities:

- Have students brainstorm as many famous bears as possible (Smokey the Bear, Winnie The Pooh, Berenstain Bears, etc.)
- Read a Winnie-The-Pooh story and have each student create a Venn diagram comparing his teddy to Winnie.
- Discuss foods that real bears eat compared to the fictional teddy bears (fish, bugs, and berries versus porridge and jam).

Whose Bear Are You?

Read *Where's My Teddy?* by Jez Alborough (Candlewick Press, 1993) and then play a listening game. In this story not only does Eddie lose his small teddy bear, Freddie, but a huge bear in the forest loses his very large bear, too. What a fright they experience when they find each other's bears! After reading, ask students to describe the bears in the story. Ask them how the bears were alike or different.

To practice listening skills, line up your teddy-bear guests in front of the classroom. Ask each child to give a few clues as to which bear belongs to him. (For example: "My bear has a rip on his left ear.") After each clue the child says, "Where's my Teddy?" and chooses a classmate to guess which bear he described. Can your students identify the mystery teddies?

Blue-Ribbon Bears

Enter students' teddy bears in a unique bear beauty contest to teach adjectives and superlatives. Give students a few minutes to observe the class bears. Then list on chart paper all the categories by which to judge the bears. Provide each student a copy of the ribbon award on page 73. Have each student write one descriptive word on a blue ribbon to award to a teddy bear. Explain that since each ribbon will only go to one bear, the descriptive word will need to have an "-est," "most," or "best" added to it. This addition will show that the bear was compared to all the other bears and won that category. Have students color and cut out the blue ribbons. To top off your "jam-bear-ee," award blue ribbons to the teddy bears. Make sure each bear receives a blue ribbon (for example: furriest, oldest,chubbiest, cutest, skinniest, biggest, tallest, tiniest, happiest, most beautiful, cleanest, most worn, newest, shortest).

Books About TEDDY BEARS

Encourage students to snuggle up with a teddy bear and a good book. Create a cozy reading den from a large appliance box. Decorate the den with plump pillows and cuddly bears.

First Flight

by David McPhail
(Little, Brown & Company;1987)

A young boy takes his teddy bear along on his first airplane trip. The boy is very well behaved, but the bear is not! After reading, discuss the bear's bad manners. Ask students if they have ever taken their bears or other stuffed animals on trips. Discuss how a familiar toy, blanket, or pillow can help one feel secure in a new place. Then make plans to take your own teddy on a trip!

With a little preparation, you can involve a class teddy bear in your lessons. Take your teddy bear on vacation! Take pictures of him as he accompanies you on your travels. Position your bear so he appears to be driving your car. Other photos may show your teddy picking up luggage at the airport, standing in front of a famous site, or dressed for a beach or ski trip. Mount the photos in a photo album titled "Teddy Bear's Travels."

Share your photo album and introduce your teddy bear to students. Have students think of adventures they can have with the bear. Where in the world would they like to go with their class teddy? How would Teddy behave? What would the bear see and do? Have each student write a story or postcard from the bear's point of view and illustrate a "photo" from the journey. Share the bear adventures and locate each bear on a map.

Ira Sleeps Over

Written & Illustrated by Bernard Waber
(Houghton Mifflin Company, 1972)

Ira is invited to his friend Reggie's house for a sleep over. There's just one problem. Should Ira take Tah Tah, his teddy bear? He has never slept without Tah Tah before. But Ira's sister warns him that Reggie will laugh at him and call him a baby. Ira has a hard time making a decision.

Before reading *Ira Sleeps Over,* prepare a simple graph. Across the top of the graph, write *Should Ira take his teddy bear?* Give each student a bear-shaped cutout and instruct him to write his name on the cutout. Begin reading the story but stop on page 11. At this point allow students to vote by placing their bear cutouts in the appropriate columns. Ask each student to give a reason why or why not Ira should take his bear. Finish reading the story and discuss the graph.

This Is The Bear
And The Picnic Lunch
by Sarah Hayes & Helen Craig
(Joy Street Books, 1989)

In this rhyming story, a young boy plans a picnic with his two good friends—his dog and his teddy bear. But they end up changing the plans slightly. Children can see what the dog and the teddy bear are thinking because they have their own thought bubbles in the pictures. After reading, discuss the difference between speech bubbles and thought bubbles. Ask what a teddy bear might be thinking as he is dragged around by a child. Brainstorm places that children might take their teddy bears such as a picnic, a camping trip, the beach, or Grandma's house. Have each child draw a picture of himself with his teddy bear in a particular situation. Have students then draw speech bubbles for themselves and thought bubbles for the bears. Collect the drawings for a class book titled, "If Teddy Bears Could Talk…"

Teddy Bear Farmer
by Phoebe and Joan Worthington
(Viking Kestrel, 1985)

In this story the reader sees a day in the life of a teddy-bear farmer from sunrise to sunset. After reading one of these books, have your students "ask" their teddy bears what they want to be when they grow up (examples: teddy-bear policeman, teddy-bear teacher). Then have each student write a short story and draw a picture about what his teddy bear wants to be. Compile the stories and pictures into a class book entitled "Teddy-Bear Careers." (These authors also wrote *Teddy Bear Coalman* and *Teddy Bear Baker*.)

Corduroy
Written & Illustrated by Don Freeman
The Viking Press, 1968

Corduroy is a classic teddy-bear story that conveys a touching message of acceptance and friendship. Lisa spots Corduroy, a stuffed bear, in the toy department of a large store. She desperately wants to buy Corduroy, but Mother points out that he is missing a button and doesn't even look new. That night, Corduroy goes on a delightful adventure searching for his button. His search is unsuccessful and Corduroy thinks he'll never have a special friend until Lisa shows up again to take him home.

After reading the book, discuss how people can also be treated badly based on outward appearances only. Then lighten the mood with a class scavenger hunt. Provide each student with a copy of the pattern on page 79. Point out that Corduroy is missing one button. Ask students to help Corduroy find his buttons. Have them look for buttons that are hidden in the classroom. (Make sure to hide more than one button per child so that everyone gets to find one.) Tell each student to find one button only and take it back to his desk. When everyone has found a button, have students color their bears and glue on the buttons. Allow each student to take his Corduroy home as a reminder of a very important lesson.

More Books About Teddies:

Jesse Bear, What Will You Wear?
by Nancy White Carlstrom
(Aladdin Paperbacks, 1986)

Teddy Bear's Moving Day
by Susanna Gretz
(Four Winds Press, 1981)

Teddy Bear Squares

Blue-Ribbon Bear

Note To The Teacher: Use the top reproducible with "Teddy-Bear Squares" on page 66, and the bottom reproducible with "Blue-Ribbon Bears" on page 70.

Name_____

The Teddy Bears' Picnic

1. Seven brown bears, three black bears, and six white bears brought baskets to the picnic. How many bears in all brought picnic baskets?

2. Twelve bears played hide-and-seek at the picnic. Seven of the bears hid in the tree. How many bears did not hide in the tree?

3. Brown Bear brought six apples, three bananas, and eight pears to the picnic. How many pieces of fruit did he bring altogether?

4. Ten white teddy bears were planning to sing a song. Two teddy bears had sore throats and couldn't sing. How many Teddy bears could sing?

5. Thirteen brown bears decided to take a nap. Only seven bears fell asleep. How many bears did not go to sleep?

6. Fifteen bears were on the green team and nine bears were on the blue team. How many more bears were on the green team than the blue team?

7. Seventeen teddy bears were swinging in the trees. Eight teddy bears jumped off. How many teddy bears were left in the trees?

8. Black Bear pulled five white teddy bears, seven brown teddy bears, and three red teddy bears in his wagon. How many teddy bears did he pull in all?

Bonus Box: Write a story about your teddy bear at the Teddy Bear's Picnic. What did he bring? What games did he play?

deserves a

BEAR HUG

for

I'm "bear-y"
proud of you!

_____
teacher

©1996 The Education Center, Inc.

**BEHAVIOR
that
"BEARS"
Reporting**

_____
is "bear-y" well-behaved!

KEEP IT UP!

_____
teacher

©1996 The Education Center, Inc. • *DECEMBER* • TEC195

To All Teddy Bears:

Please come to our Teddy Bears' Fair!

date: _____

time: _____

place: _____

(Bring a friend.)

©1996 The Education Center, Inc. • *DECEMBER* • TEC195

Nametags for Teddy Bears

A "Bear-y" Special Visitor

_____ 's Bear,

_____

©1996 The Education Center, Inc. • *DECEMBER* • TEC195

Patterns
Use with "ABC Bears" on page 62 and
"News That Bears Repeating!" on page 65.

Pattern
Use with "Cinnamon Bears" on page 65,
and "Teddy-Bear Squares," "Teddy Phonics," and "Superteddy Tales" on page 66.

Patterns
Use with "Stuffed Teddy Bears" on page 64.

A Winter Wonderland

"Snow" joke! This collection of cross-curricular activities will warm up your classroom!

by Amy Barsanti and Stacie Stone Davis

White Wonderful Winter

Start your winter unit on a warm note by sharing the book *White Wonderful Winter!* by Elaine W. Good (Good Books®, 1994). Then use this book as a springboard for a brainstorming session that will result in a list of winter-related words. Draw lines on your blackboard to create five sections. Assign each section a category such as winter events, winter animals, winter activities, winter sports, winter clothing, etc. Ask students to name winter-related words that belong to each category. After each student responds, write his word in the appropriate section on the blackboard.

When the brainstorming session is over, give each student a copy of the poetry pattern on page 91. Challenge each student to write a winter poem using the class-generated list to help him. Have volunteers share their completed poems; then staple the poems to a bulletin board that has been covered with blue construction paper and decorated with green construction-paper pine trees. Add a title strip that says "White Wonderful Winter" and you've got yourself a cozy winter display.

Snow ___is falling___,
Animals ___are hiding___.
White wonderful winter!
Grown-ups ___shoveling___,
Kids ___sledding___.
White wonderful winter!
by
Blake

Snow People

Spruce up your bulletin board with these life-size snow people. To make them, divide students into pairs; then give each student a length of white bulletin-board paper that is slightly longer than his height. Have one member from each pair lie down atop his bulletin-board paper. Using a pencil, each student's partner traces his outline on the sheet of bulletin-board paper. Repeat this process for the other member of each student pair. Afterward have each student cut out his shape. Then have each student embellish the resulting shape with construction-paper features and clothing so that it resembles a snowman. Secure the snowmen to the walls near the "White Wonderful Winter" bulletin board.

WHITE WONDERFUL WINTER

Snow Is Falling

Read the book *Snow Is Falling* by Franklyn
M. Branley (Harper & Row, 1986) to help students learn more about the characteristics, benefits, and hazards associated with snow. Then
tell students that snowflakes vary widely in size
and in shape. Although no two snowflakes are
exactly the same, all snowflakes have six sides.
Then, on a snowy day, head outdoors so that
students can examine snowflakes. To prepare
for this activity, place a sheet of black construction paper for each child in a freezer. Just before going outside, give each child one of the
sheets of construction paper and a small magnifying glass. Have the student catch a snowflake
on his paper, then use the magnifying glass to
examine the snowflake. Repeat this process as
time permits.

After you've returned to the classroom, have
students draw likenesses of their snowflakes on
white, three-inch construction-paper squares.
Have students draw a winter scene on a length
of bulletin-board paper and glue their squares to
the resulting mural.

From Snow To Water

Snow is an important source of water. Explain
that even though snow contains much less water than rain, melted snow provides water for
electric power plants, irrigation reservoirs,
streams, and wells. Tell students that the water
contained in six inches of wet snow equals the
water contained in one inch of rain.

Then engage students in this melting activity.
Put a desired amount of snow in a large, clear
plastic container. Challenge students to estimate how long it will take the snow to melt; then
write their guesses on a sheet of chart paper.
Next have each student guess how much water
will be in the container once the snow melts. To
do this, have each student in turn use a permanent felt-tip marker to draw a line on the container indicating how much water he thinks will
be in the container once the snow melts. To
eliminate confusion, have each child write his
initials next to his line. After the snow melts,
compare students' estimates to the actual melting time and amount of water in the container.
Afterward pour the melted snow into a watering
can and have a volunteer water your classroom
plants.

Snow As An Insulator

Students may be surprised to learn that snow is considered an *insulator*. Explain that an insulator helps keep heat in a specific area. Give students examples of things that are insulated. For example, explain that most homes are insulated so that heat does not leave the structure during cold weather or enter the structure during warmer weather. Then show students a Thermos® bottle filled with hot tea. Open the bottle and explain that since it is insulated, the tea is very warm. Explain to students that the inner container of the Thermos® bottle contains a type of glass that is a poor conductor of heat.

Then use this experiment to give students a better understanding of how snow actually protects plants and hibernating animals from the cold winter air. For this experiment you will need two thermometers and two dishpans. Fill each dishpan with snow and set the dishpans outside your window. Put one thermometer in a dishpan atop the snow. Bury the second thermometer in the other snow-filled dishpan. Then, one hour later, remove the thermometers and read the temperatures. Compare the temperatures; then ask students to discuss what the warmer temperature on the buried thermometer means in terms of plants and animals seeking warmth during winter months.

Record Snowfall

Compare record snowfalls for measurement practice. According to the *Guinness Book Of World Records*, the greatest snowfall in a 24-hour period is 78 inches of snow. This record was set at Mile 47 Camp, Cooper River Division, Alaska. Just how much snow is 78 inches? Use this activity to find out. Begin by cutting a 78-inch length of string. Use masking tape to secure the string to a wall as shown. Allow each student in turn to stand next to the string and compare his height to the snow depth. After each student has had a turn, survey students to find out how many of them would enjoy having 78 inches of snow fall at their homes and what they would do in all that snow.

If desired, cut lengths of string to represent other record snowfalls (see the chart for assistance). In turn put each length of string on the floor. Have each student lie down next to the string to compare his height to that of the snowfall.

Record Snowfalls
For a 12-month period: 1,224 1/2 in.
For a single snowstorm: 189 in.
For a 24-hour period: 78 in.
Greatest depth of snow: 37 ft., 7 in.

Snow Day!

No doubt, if 78 inches of snow were to fall in your students' hometowns, there might just be one or two school closings. Share the story *Snow Day* by Betsy Maestro (Scholastic Inc., 1989) to give your students a better understanding of the work involved in clearing snow from different areas after a snowstorm. Afterward have the head of the highway department visit your classroom to talk about snow removal. Encourage students to ask questions like, "How long does it take to plow the city's (town's, village's) roads?" and, "How do you decide which roads to plow first?"

Afterward have each student write a news report about the day it snowed 78 inches in 24 hours. Allow students to illustrate their stories; then staple the completed projects to a bulletin board titled "Snow Day!"

Snowed In

For a comparison on how times have changed, share the story *Snowed In* by Barbara M. Lucas (Bradbury Press, 1993). This story details how plenty of paper, pencils, and books help one Wyoming family deal with winter. After reading, share your childhood memories of winter and particularly harsh blizzards; then ask students to do the same. Next have students brainstorm a list of things that people might do nowadays if they got snowed in. Then repeat this process, asking students to name things people may have done in the olden days when they were snowed in. Compare the lists; then survey students to find out how many of them would enjoy spending winter the old-fashioned way. Conclude the lesson by asking each student to pretend that he is one of the storybook characters. Have each student write a story called "The Winter Of 1915" on a sheet of notebook paper; then bind the completed stories in a classroom collection titled "Snowed In."

Snowman Poem

One outdoor activity that's a favorite among youngsters is building snowmen. Read the story *Bob The Snowman* by Sylvia Loretan and Jan Lenica (Scholastic Inc., 1993). After reading, discuss what happened to Bob and briefly explain the water cycle. Then teach your students this fun snowman poem. If desired, have student groups visit other classrooms and read the poem to those students.

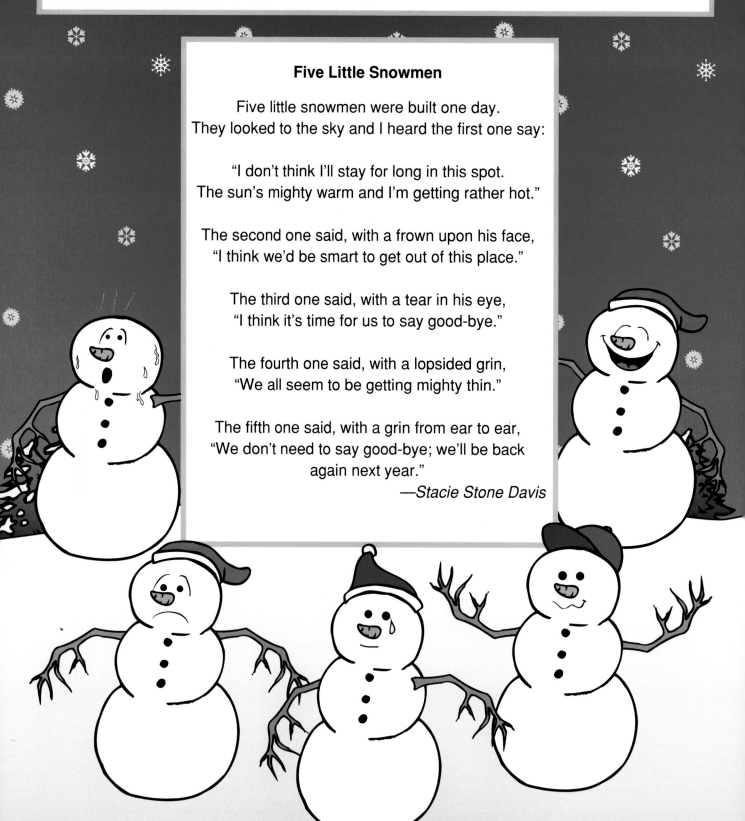

Five Little Snowmen

Five little snowmen were built one day.
They looked to the sky and I heard the first one say:

"I don't think I'll stay for long in this spot.
The sun's mighty warm and I'm getting rather hot."

The second one said, with a frown upon his face,
"I think we'd be smart to get out of this place."

The third one said, with a tear in his eye,
"I think it's time for us to say good-bye."

The fourth one said, with a lopsided grin,
"We all seem to be getting mighty thin."

The fifth one said, with a grin from ear to ear,
"We don't need to say good-bye; we'll be back
again next year."
—*Stacie Stone Davis*

Winter-Sports Fun:
A Choral Reading

Teach your students this choral reading to introduce them to some different types of winter recreation. Divide students into five groups: a skiers group, an ice-skaters group, a luge group, an ice fishers group, and a showshoers group. Provide each student with a copy of the choral reading below. Allow students to wear hats, scarves, or mittens while performing the choral reading. If desired, after practicing, have students present the choral reading for classmates and parents.

All:
In the winter there's so much that you can do.
So join us and find a sport that interests you.

Skiers:
On two straight boards we swish and glide,
Down a huge mountain or a big hillside.

Ice-skaters:
We spin, we jump, and we make figure eights.
It's wonderful to be on the ice in our skates.

Lugers:
We get on our sleds and lie on our backs.
Then we slide down the steep, icy tracks.

Ice fishers:
We drill through the ice, then drop in our bait.
We try to stay warm while for fish we wait.

Snowshoers:
We strap on our shoes and walk among the trees,
Looking for rabbits, deer, and little chickadees.

All:
So put on your coat and hat, and get outside.
Winter's a time for fun—don't stay indoors and hide!
—*Stacie Stone Davis*

Snow Fun

Try this graphing idea. Ask students to name winter activities in which they like to participate. List students' responses on the board. Then, on a large sheet of chart paper, draw a graph as shown. Ask each student to decide which activity she likes best; then mark it on the graph. After each student has had a turn, discuss the results of the graph with students.

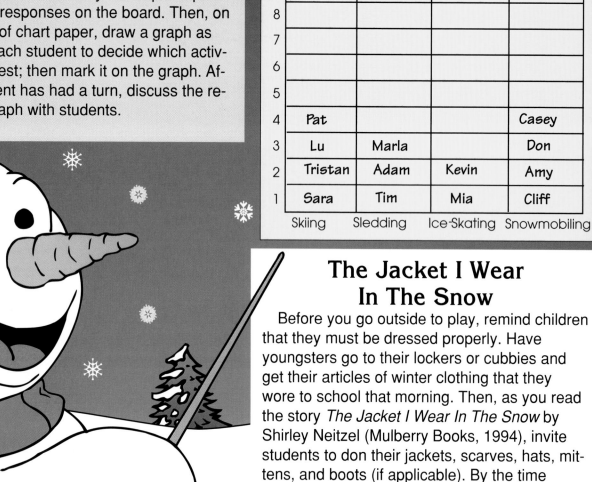

	Skiing	Sledding	Ice-Skating	Snowmobiling
10				
9				
8				
7				
6				
5				
4	Pat			Casey
3	Lu	Marla		Don
2	Tristan	Adam	Kevin	Amy
1	Sara	Tim	Mia	Cliff

The Jacket I Wear In The Snow

Before you go outside to play, remind children that they must be dressed properly. Have youngsters go to their lockers or cubbies and get their articles of winter clothing that they wore to school that morning. Then, as you read the story *The Jacket I Wear In The Snow* by Shirley Neitzel (Mulberry Books, 1994), invite students to don their jackets, scarves, hats, mittens, and boots (if applicable). By the time you've finished the story, students will be dressed and ready to head out the door to play some of the games described on page 87!

It's A Winter Fest!

"Snow" time like now for a Winter Festival. Pick a nice winter day to go outside and celebrate with these games and activities. If you live in an area that doesn't get much snow, substitute Styrofoam® balls for snowballs—and have fun!

The Mitten Relay

Try this fun relay race to get students moving on a cold winter day. Begin by dividing the class into four teams. Provide the first member of each team with a scarf and a pair of mittens. To play, the first member of each team puts on the scarf and mittens at the sound of a signal, runs to a predetermined spot, and then runs back to his team members. The first runner then removes the scarf and mittens and gives them to the next team member, who then runs to the predetermined spot and back. The first team to have all of its members complete the race wins.

Snowball Toss

This fun game emphasizes gross-motor practice. To play, divide students into four teams. Give one volunteer from each team a Hula-Hoop®. Have the student holding the Hula-Hoop® stand a desired distance from his teammates, facing them as shown. In turn each team member takes a chance at throwing a snowball through the Hula-Hoop®. Each member who throws the snowball through the hoop earns a point for his team. The team with the most points at the end of the game wins!

A Snow Throw

Hold a Snow Throw with your students. Begin by making a large *X* in the snow. In turn allow each child to throw a snowball. Tell each student to throw his snowball as close to the *X* as possible. When the game is over, give the child whose snowball is the closest to the *X* a prize. If desired, hand out other silly prizes, such as a prize for the snowball that was thrown the shortest distance or for the snowball that was thrown the greatest distance beyond the *X*.

Treats For A Cold Day

When students return indoors, they'll be ready for something in their tummies. Try these recipes to make some yummy treats; then settle down with a good book together.

Warm-Your-Insides Fruit Punch

You'll need:

1 bottle cranberry juice (48 oz.)
1 can pineapple juice (46 oz.)
1 bottle orange-pineapple juice (46 oz.)
1/2 cup brown sugar
1/4 teaspoon salt
large Crock-Pot®
spoon
ladle
Styrofoam® cups (one for each student)
cinnamon sticks (optional)

Pour the first five ingredients into the Crock-Pot®. Bring the mixture to a boil; then let it simmer for 30 minutes. Remove it from the heat and let it cool. Ladle some of the fruit drink into each cup and serve it with a cinnamon stick if desired.

"Snow-Covered" Snack Mix

You'll need:

1 package yogurt-covered peanuts
1 package yogurt-covered pretzels
mixing bowl
spoon
resealable plastic bags (one for each student)

Combine the first two ingredients in the mixing bowl. Spoon a portion of the mix into a resealable plastic bag for each student.

Cozy Up With A Good Book And Read!
Try these activities for an avalanche of wintertime fun.

North Country Night
by Daniel San Souci
(Bantam Doubleday Dell Books
For Young Readers, 1994)

This picture book details the habits and the hardships of woodland creatures on a snowy night. It is a realistic portrayal, full of descriptive language. The nighttime setting is compelling and the illustrations are exquisite.

After sharing this book with students, ask them to recall animals from the story. Have students name each animal and the activities in which each animal was involved. List students' responses on the board. Afterward discuss the descriptive language found in the story.

Then have each student make his own winter picture similar to the illustrations found in the book. Give each student a 12" x 18" sheet of blue construction paper. Have each student use crayons to draw a nighttime winter scene on his sheet of paper. Afterward have each student use a spray bottle that has been filled with diluted white tempera paint to spritz his paper to look like snow. Encourage each student to write a story about his picture using as much descriptive language as possible. Staple the completed pictures and stories to a bulletin board titled "North Country Night."

Elmer In The Snow
by David McKee
(Lothrop, Lee & Shepard Books; 1995)

In this story Elmer, the patchwork elephant, leads his elephant friends on a journey to a place where they find snow to play in. After reading the book, discuss with students the things that they like to do in the snow; then let each student make his own Elmer picture. Give each student a construction-paper copy of the elephant pattern on page 92. Encourage each student to use a variety of crayons to color his elephant to make him appear to be patchwork. Then have each student cut out his elephant. Next—using the patchwork elephant as a template—have each student trace several elephant shapes onto a piece of 12" x 18" gray construction paper and then cut out the elephant shapes. If desired, also have each child make a snow elephant by tracing an elephant on white construction paper, then cutting it out. Have each student glue all of his elephants to a 12" x 18" sheet of light blue construction paper. Encourage each student to use crayons to draw a winter scene around the elephants. Have each child complete his picture by adding snowflakes to the scene. These snowflakes can be made by repeatedly dipping a Q-tip® cotton swab into a shallow container of white tempera paint and then dotting it onto the construction paper. Display the completed projects on a bulletin board titled "Adventures With Elmer."

Hopper
by Marcus Pfister
(North-South Books, Inc.; 1991)

In this story, Hopper the snowshoe hare enjoys wintertime adventures with his friend Nick and his mother. After reading the story, discuss how the *protective coloration* of snowshoe rabbits helps protect them.

Then have each student make her own Hopper snowshoe hare. To make a hare, have each student glue two cotton balls together to form the body. Then have her cut a cotton swab in half and glue the pieces behind the body to resemble ears. Complete the hare by having the student glue on two wiggle eyes and add final details with a fine-point felt-tip marker.

Then have each student make a winter-scene diorama, of which Hopper will be a part. Glue the hare to the inside of a shoebox. Provide students with art materials—such as construction paper, tissue paper, glue, scissors, and glitter—that they can use to complete their winter scenes.

Warm Your Hearts With A Book

Winter by Ron Hirschi (Puffin Books, 1996)
Sadie And The Snowman by Allen Morgan
   (Scholastic Inc., 1987)
Annie And The Wild Animals by Jan Brett
   (The Trumpet Club, 1992)
Winter Rabbit by Patrick Yee
   (Puffin Books, 1996)
Reuben And The Blizzard by Merle Good
   (Good Books®, 1995)

Snow _____,
Animals _____.
White wonderful winter!
Grown-ups _____,
Kids _____.
White wonderful winter!
by

_____

Elephant Pattern

Use with *Elmer In The Snow* on page 89.

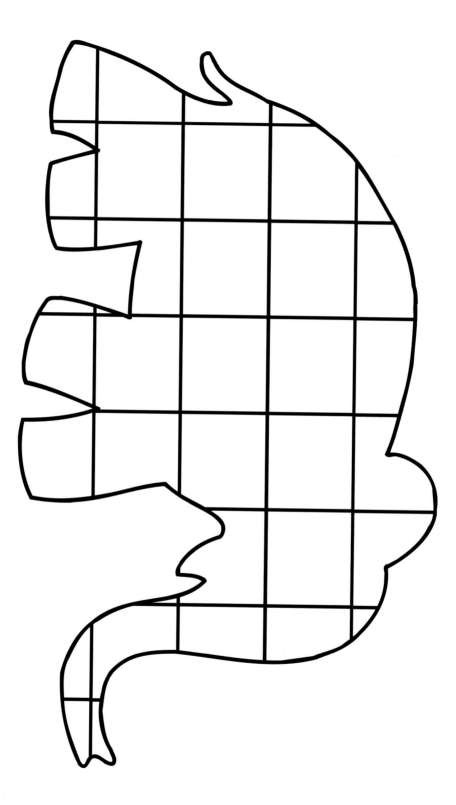

Name _____ *Problem solving*

Fun With Snowmen

Directions:
1. Cut out the snowmen below.
2. Color each snowman's hat.
3. Use the snowmen to solve the problems.

Put your snowmen in a row. Color the hats to show how you arranged your snowmen. Can you do this five more times?

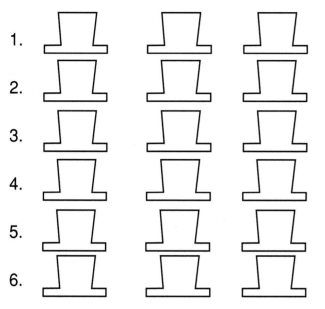

1.

2.

3.

4.

5.

6.

One day the three snowmen had a race. Use the clues and your snowmen cutouts to help you fill in the chart.
Clue 1—The snowman with the blue hat was behind the snowman with the yellow hat.
Clue 2—The snowman with the red hat was not first.
Clue 3—The snowman with the blue hat was in front of the snowman with the red hat.

	First	Second	Third
Red snowman			
Yellow snowman			
Blue snowman			

©1996 The Education Center, Inc. • *DECEMBER* • TEC195

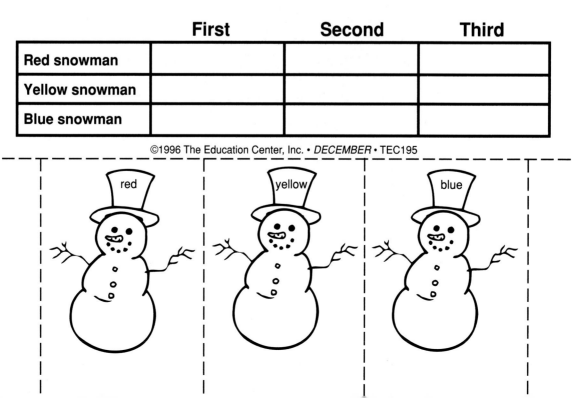

red   yellow   blue

Marvelous Mittens

Try these magnificent mitten activities on for size.

ideas by Stacie Stone Davis

Mittens By The Mantel

Here's a center that students will return to again and again. Sponge-paint a sheet of poster board to look like a fireplace. Glue construction-paper flames and logs to the inside of the fireplace. Cut a length of brown bulletin-board paper and then glue it to the top of the poster-board fireplace to serve as a mantel. Then staple a length of yarn from one end of the mantle to the other. Attach a supply of mittens to the string with clothespins. Inside each mitten tuck a slip of paper on which an activity is printed (see the suggestions below); then hang the fireplace where students can reach it easily. When a child has free time invite him to select an activity from one of the mittens. Provide the student with the materials he needs; then let him complete the activity.

Make a list of things (besides mittens) that come in pairs.

Practice your addition facts using some mitten cutouts to help you.

Write a story about a time you lost a mitten in the snow.

Write a story about an animal that makes its home inside your mitten.

List five objects that could fit inside a mitten.

Mitten Measurement

Measuring mittens is the perfect way to introduce non-standard units. Make several construction-paper copies of the mitten patterns on page 96. Cut out the mittens and store them in a resealable bag. Place the bag at a center and have students use the mitten cutouts to determine lengths of items and distances—in mittens! Wow, my desk is six mittens long!

Mixed-Up Mittens

Students will give their thumbs-up sign of approval to this fun patterning activity. Give each student a white construction-paper copy of the mitten patterns on page 96. Invite the student to decorate the mittens so that when they are placed side by side, they form a pattern. For example, students could decorate one mitten with stars and the next mitten with stripes; then repeat the process until he has no more mitten cutouts left. Next have each student cut his mittens out. Give each student a resealable plastic bag in which to place his cutouts; then put all the bags at a center so that students can use them for patterning practice during free time.

Count By Twos

Two, four, six, eight; this counting activity is really great! Ask each student to bring a pair of mittens from home. Select several volunteers to put on their mittens and then come to the front of the room. As the children hold up their hands, practice counting by twos. Challenge older students by asking them to each bring in a pair of gloves. Use the gloves to practice counting by fives.

Mitten Match

This fun math game is sure to be enjoyed by all your students. Give each child a copy of a gameboard similar to the one shown. Have each child program each square on the gameboard with a number. (A number may be used more than once.) To play, give each child a supply of minimarshmallows to use as snowball markers. Then call out a math problem. The student determines the answer to the math problem; then, if he has the corresponding answer on his gameboard, he covers that spot. (If a child has two squares programmed with the same number, he may only cover one space. The student must wait until another math problem with that sum is called before he can cover the other space.) The first child to have one horizontal or vertical row covered wins.

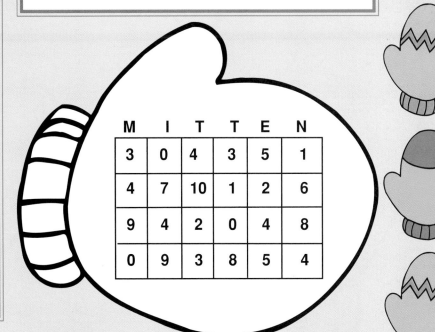

M	I	T	T	E	N
3	0	4	3	5	1
4	7	10	1	2	6
9	4	2	0	4	8
0	9	3	8	5	4

Mitten Patterns
Use with the activities on pages 94 and 95.

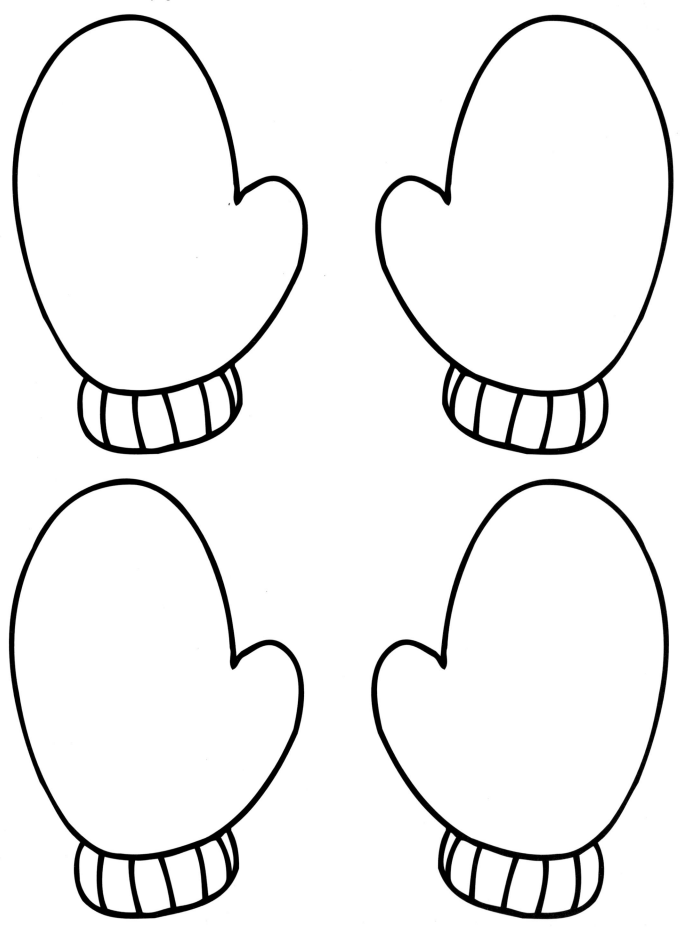